DATE DUE

Historians on the Homefront

Historians on the Homefront

AMERICAN PROPAGANDISTS

FOR THE GREAT WAR

George T. Blakey

The University Press of Kentucky

Standard Book Number: 8131-1236-2

Library of Congress Catalog Card Number: 79-132825

Copyright © 1970 by The University Press of Kentucky

A statewide cooperative scholarly publishing agency
serving Berea College, Centre College of Kentucky,
Eastern Kentucky University, Kentucky State College,
Morehead State University, Murray State University,
University of Kentucky, University of Louisville,
and Western Kentucky University.

Editorial and Sales Offices: Lexington, Kentucky 40506

To the guidance of John E. Wiltz
and the friendship of the Eastern Indiana Center,
I owe my deepest thanks

Contents

I. The Dilemma of War

As America entered war in April 1917, two historians issued appeals for support and service during the national crisis: President Woodrow Wilson and his former professor, J. Franklin Jameson. Wilson asked for mobilization of America's physical resources to wage a moral crusade against the forces of teutonic militarism in Europe. Jameson sought to muster the intellectual resources of historians in defense of America's position. The appeals of these two men presented in microcosm the dilemma facing America's young historical profession, that of how far a historian could go in patriotic support of his nation's war aims and still remain faithful to the canons of scholarship. In a period of national crisis would it be possible to serve both profession and country, one demanding scholarly detachment, the other emotional commitment?

Wilson's appeal came less from a historian than from the leader of world democracy; he aimed it at the public rather than the academic community and sought an emotional rather than an intellectual response. Although he had earned his doctorate in history at Johns Hopkins University, had written several volumes of historical narrative and biography, and had taught at several schools including Princeton, where he had also served as president, Wilson did not regard himself as primarily a professional scholar. Once he left the academic world for politics, he channeled his energies into the New Jersey governorship and then the American presidency more enthusiastically than he had into scholarly work. Early in his career he had indicated his predilections when he wrote to his fiancee, "I have no patience for the tedious toil of what is known as 'research'; I have a passion for interpreting great thoughts to the world; I should be complete if I could inspire a great movement of opinion, if I could read the experiences of the past into the practical life of the men of today."[1]

His war message allowed him to do just this. By reading the experiences of the past into present circumstances he could present a more forceful case for taking America into a European war. The packed galleries of the House of Representatives, the assembled congressmen, cabinet members, Supreme Court justices, and diplomatic corps all anticipated his remarks on that evening of April 2. Gripping the typewritten pages of his address in both hands and occasionally resting an arm on the green baize-covered lectern, the historian-turned-president marshalled his interpretation of the recent past into an indictment of bad faith, broken promises, and barbarism and declared that a state of war existed with the German government. America had no choice but to defend its honor; "God helping her, she can do no other." His secretary of state later recalled that when the president finished "the vast audience broke into a tumult of applause that was deafening. They clapped, they stamped, they cheered," they waved flags and gave the president a standing ovation.[2] Raising flags and cheers proved an easier task than raising a nation to readiness for war, but Wilson's message had asked for more than enthusiasm and loyalty. It demanded organization of the nation's strength to fight the enemies of democracy and reestablish the proper balance of power in Europe, and historians would judge Wilson for his success or failure in prosecuting the war, not for his abdication from the scholarly world.

In contrast to Wilson's appeal for national mobilization, Jameson's was that of a professional historian directed to his colleagues in the academic field. If historians could have considered anyone their unofficial leader in 1917, it probably would have been Jameson. He seemed older than his fifty-eight years, partly because of his courtly manners and shyness; his rimless glasses and neatly trimmed gray beard accentuated his age, and his slender form and conservative suits added to his patriarchal aura. As a tribute to his standing, his associates had elected him president of the American Historical Association in 1907, and invitations to

[1] Wilson to Ellen Axson, 24 February 1885, in Arthur Link, ed., *The Papers of Woodrow Wilson* (Princeton, 1968), 4:287.
[2] Robert Lansing, *War Memoirs of Robert Lansing* (Indianapolis, 1935), p. 242.

his annual "convivium historicum" in Branford, Connecticut, soon became coveted items. An exhortation from Jameson undoubtedly had more effect than that from any other historian because his career symbolized the growth and professionalization of the young community of historical scholars in the United States. Recipient of the first Ph.D. in history from Johns Hopkins in 1882, he had remained there to help shape the university's historical seminar, the young Woodrow Wilson being one of his early students in 1883. He then moved on to teach at Brown University and later to become head of the history department at the University of Chicago. Long before the war Jameson had placed researchers in his debt for his tireless efforts in compiling and publishing bibliographies and guides to manuscript collections and archives. In 1917, in addition to his duties as director of historical research at the Carnegie Institution in Washington, he was managing editor of the *American Historical Review*, a position he had held since its founding in 1895, with the exception of the years 1901-1905.[3]

Shortly after his illustrious student's war message, Jameson began recruiting historians for war service. He used the pages of the *Review* as a vehicle for his formal keynote in presenting the case for the scholar's participation in the war. The academic scientist, he pointed out, could find his wartime role with ease. "He can invent a new range-finder or a new explosive. He can improve the quality of optical glass. He can seek new sources of potash. He can make two potatoes grow where one grew before." But the place of the historian seemed more remote, less essential to the national crisis. "Against such an opinion the mind of the virile historical student protests with all his might. What is more essential to the successful prosecution of a great national war than an enlightened, unified, and powerfully-acting public opinion? . . . But how can public opinion be enlightened, homogeneous, and powerful, in a crisis which is in the plainest way

---

[3] A full-length biography of Jameson has yet to be written, but the most inclusive treatment of his life can be found in the collection of essays edited by Ruth Anna Fisher and William L. Fox, *J. Franklin Jameson: A Tribute* (Washington, D.C., 1965).

the product of historic forces if it is not informed in facts and lessons of history?" Jameson urged historians to abandon their cloisters and use their knowledge "energetically and boldly" for the good of the nation. Historians had an obligation not only to national service, but to history, for "if the public is not guided by sound historical information, it will be guided by unsound."[4]

Wilson's and Jameson's calls to arms constituted a crusade which necessitated a dual response from receptive historians. One appealed to the patriotism and service of American citizens for defeating the enemies of America; the other appealed to scholarly talents in the historical profession for homogenizing American opinion. Both presented historians with a task which required the temporary relinquishment of scholarly ideals such as detachment, objectivity, and a dispassionate approach to recent historical events. The concurrent dilemma was apparent to this community of professional scholars hardly a generation old. The struggle to create this profession had been at the expense of traditional, patriotic historians whose scholarly training had been casual and erratic, whose careers were generally nonacademic, and whose work aimed as much at inspiring national pride as at uncovering historical truth. Responding to the war effort might mean the capitulation of the new professional historians to their amateur counterparts, whom they had only recently defeated for the leadership of the historical community.

This dilemma would not have been so serious had the profession been older and more firmly established. Not until 1884, however, did American historians formally constitute a profession apart from other scholarly disciplines and casual organizations, and memories of the struggle for leadership between academics and amateurs were still fresh. It was in September of that year that forty members of the Social Science Association met in a small parlor of the United States Hotel in Saratoga, New York, and drew up a charter founding the American Historical Association. Less than one-third of the charter members were trained historians,

    [4] John Franklin Jameson, "Historical Scholars in Wartime," *American Historical Review* (hereafter cited as *AHR*) 22 (July 1917): 831-33.

but this assemblage had gathered at the prompting of such university professors as Herbert Baxter Adams of Johns Hopkins, Moses Coit Tyler of Cornell, and Charles Kendall Adams of the University of Michigan. This "inner circle" of scholars was instrumental in awarding the first presidency to Andrew D. White, who had helped introduce graduate history instruction at Michigan and Cornell.[5] Despite the professional stature of the new organization, nonacademic historians maintained a majority of the membership and dominated its activities for several more years. Numerical disparity between the two groups made this situation almost inevitable. There were probably no more than twenty men devoted to full-time history teaching in American colleges and universities in 1884, and of those "there were hardly two that knew more than one or two of the others."[6]

In the same year as the founding of the American Historical Association, Harvard University's chief librarian, Justin Winsor, began editing his eight-volume *Narrative and Critical History of America*. This monumental compilation of essays, maps, annotated bibliographies, and guides to archives and manuscript collections long remained a publishing landmark and a standard research aid for students of history. Still, it was ironic that professional historians exerted so little influence upon it. Of the thirty-nine authors who contributed material only two were full-time professors of history; the remainder were librarians, writers, nonacademic historians and antiquarians, and professors of divinity, law, mathematics, paleontology, and other subjects. This composite-author history paralleled the situation that existed in the new American Historical Association in the latter part of the nineteenth century —talented amateurs still dominated the field.

Henry Adams and Francis Parkman typified these amateurs. Largely self-educated in historical technique, these men received various sobriquets such as patricians, romantics, and apologists to

5 [Herbert Baxter Adams], "Secretary's Report of the Organization and Proceedings, Saratoga, September 9-10, 1884," *Papers of the American Historical Association, 1884,* 1:5-44.

6 American Historical Association, *Historical Scholarship in America: Needs and Opportunities* (New York, 1932), p. 7. Jameson wrote the introduction to this committee report.

characterize their family backgrounds, epic writing styles, and political sympathies. Adams's account of the Jefferson and Madison administrations and Parkman's volumes on the colonial explorations and wars both revealed that their authors had undertaken intensive travel and research before producing their heroic panoramas. Others such as George Bancroft spent many years in politics and diplomacy and Bancroft's massive *History of the United States* displayed his democratic bias and his almost religious commitment to American nationalism. John Fiske and James Ford Rhodes conformed to this general norm of amateur scholars whose comfortable means allowed them to travel and write at their leisure and for their own interest. Fiske lectured widely on American culture while being supported by wealthy benefactors, and Rhodes retired from a prosperous Cleveland industrial firm to study and write about the Civil War era. These men and many of their contemporaries wrote competent, sometimes distinctive, histories and still command respect for the scope and quality of their endeavors. But none of them, with the possible exception of Henry Adams, who taught briefly at Harvard, were academic historians devoted to furthering a profession and training new scholars in systematic research, writing, and publication. Despite the dominance of these men in the field, Henry Adams confided to Parkman as early as 1884, "The more I write, the more confident I feel that before long a new school of history will rise which will leave us antiquated."[7]

Adams predicted correctly, for by the turn of the century the academic historians had begun to exert a growing influence on organized historical activities and by the time of America's entry into the war in 1917, they had taken the leadership in both numbers and prestige. A good index of the shift from the amateurs to the professionals appears in the growth of graduate historical training in American universities. Before the establishment of the Johns Hopkins graduate program in 1876 advanced training in the United States was little more than a suggestion. Almost without exception American scholars had to travel and study in European, mainly

[7] 21 December 1884, in Harold Dean Cater, ed., *Henry Adams and His Friends: A Collection of His Unpublished Letters* (Boston, 1947), p. 34.

German, universities to receive a doctorate in history. Following the Johns Hopkins example several American schools developed their own graduate programs and the exodus for foreign degrees declined while an indigenous American historical profession grew proportionately. In the five-year span from 1881 to 1885 only five American schools granted doctorates in history; this had grown to twenty-two by 1915. Whereas these schools granted only 9 doctorates during the preceding half-decade, 135 students received the degree in the comparable span between 1911 and 1915. By general estimate there were approximately 500 holders of the history doctorate living in the United States in 1915, perhaps 75 percent of whose degrees had been earned in America.[8]

The style of graduate history instruction also set apart the professionals from the nonprofessionals. Using the seminar method of studying source materials and subjecting the finished product to group criticism, these new scholars underwent training in critical research and dispassionate writing. Their goal of discovering historical truth from the original sources emulated the German tradition popularized by the father of "scientific history," Leopold von Ranke, who urged students to write history "wie es eigentlich gewesen ist" (as it actually happened), free of personal interpretation by the historian. Johns Hopkins's graduate history program became a prototype which other American universities soon imitated. Herbert Baxter Adams, an American scholar who had taken his training in German universities, organized the program and during the decade 1882-1892 produced thirty-eight doctoral students, including Jameson, Wilson, and Frederick Jackson Turner. Adams would gather his students around the large red table in the history "seminary room" of Bluntschli Library and direct their attention to a research paper that a student had prepared after examining city or institutional records and manuscripts. The ensuing criticism of the paper appeared to be as important as the paper itself, and Jameson once remarked that

8 William B. Hesseltine and Louis Kaplan, "Doctors of Philosophy in History: A Statistical Study," *AHR* 47 (July 1942): 772-73; Dexter Perkins and John L. Snell, *The Education of Historians in the United States* (New York, 1962), pp. 16-17.

Wilson's ability at critical discussion and academic debate provoked his envy.[9]

The Rankean ideal of reconstructing the past from original sources and subjecting it to the scrutiny of other disinterested scholars spread from Adams's "seminary room" across the nation. Turner, for example, carried the method to Wisconsin and one of his early students recalled how Turner had impressed upon his students that original sources were the key to accuracy in relating past events. That particular student intentionally omitted any secondary sources from his research project and never forgot Turner's verdict, "So *you* are the authority."[10] Historians emerging from these new forges of formal training began to dominate the profession partly from their growing numbers and partly from the respect they commanded from their nonacademic contemporaries.

This transfer of influence manifested itself in the increasing professionalization of historical activities at the turn of the century. Annual gatherings of the American Historical Association were held with greater frequency at university cities—New Haven, Cambridge, Ann Arbor, Madison—than in metropolitan areas; fewer nonacademic historians won election to the presidency; papers delivered at these yearly sessions assumed a more scholarly level, replacing earlier antiquarian and popular presentations.[11] The appearance of the *American Historical Review* as an independent journal in 1895 signaled a further shift away from the amateurs. With Jameson as managing editor presiding over an editorial board heavily weighted with technically trained scholars and university professors, the nonacademics found themselves without an effective medium of publication. When the association gradually began to subsidize the *Review* and officially incorporated it within the organization in 1915, the creative leadership of the professionals achieved formal recognition. The founding of the Mississippi Valley Historical Association in 1907 gave testimony

[9] Henry Wilkinson Bragdon, *Woodrow Wilson: The Academic Years* (Cambridge, Mass., 1967), pp. 105-10.

[10] Guy Stanton Ford, *On and Off the Campus* (Minneapolis, 1938), p. 10.

[11] The *Annual Reports* of the association offer chronological witness to this transformation.

to this same power shift as the increased number and scholarly prestige of the professors took the lead from untrained regional historians. The mvha's largely academic officers and its scholarly journal, established in 1914, both reflected the widening gap between the professionals and the nonprofessionals. One historiographer has designated the creation of this second professional society as a turning point: "the formative era in the creation of the American historical profession was over. The patrician historians, with very few exceptions, had either retired from the scene or subsided into ineffectual antiquarianism."[12]

When Albert Bushnell Hart of Harvard began editing the *American Nation* series in 1904, the credentials of the participating authors symbolized the completion of this transfer of leadership. Although the series differed in format from Winsor's *Narrative and Critical History*, begun in 1884, its comprehensive scope and composite-author approach made it an obvious source of comparison. During the time elapsed between these two publishing events a new generation of trained historians had emerged. Whereas Winsor's thirty-nine contributors had included only two college history professors, no less than twenty of Hart's twenty-four historians were academically trained and employed. Henry Adams's prophecy of 1884 had almost come to pass; he and his amateur friends were not entirely antiquated but they were surely outnumbered by the time America entered World War I.

War in Europe had been preparing the historians' dilemma even before American entry. Historians disagreed among themselves on America's relationship to the belligerents and had divided on the part that scholars should play if the country became involved in the struggle. The diversity of opinion among historians concerning both issues reflected the division and uncertainties throughout the nation. Pacifists and German-Americans at one extreme and preparedness militants and interventionists at the other had created an abrasive counterpoint since late 1914. Marching up one side of the American street might be Jane Addams leading a chorus of "I didn't raise my boy to be a soldier," while

[12] John Higham and others, *History* (Englewood Cliffs, N. J., 1965), p. 19.

parading down the other side could be grizzled Henry Watterson, who ended his *Courier Journal* editorials with "To Hell with the Hapsburgs and the Hohenzollerns!" No sooner had fighting begun than Bernadotte Schmitt of Western Reserve accused Germany of predicating this "midsummer madness" which culminated years of German military and imperial desires.[13] William E. Dodd of Chicago shared this condemnation of German aggressiveness and told his wife that he was "almost ashamed that I have my doctorate from such a people."[14] John Burgess, who had only recently retired from Columbia, came quickly to Germany's defense with two hurriedly written books arguing that many European nations shared the guilt for the outbreak of hostilities, and that Americans should not allow current passions to diminish their appreciation of Germany's innumerable contributions to Western culture.[15]

As the carnage of the European war mounted through 1915-1916 and American neutrality became more rhetoric than reality, the scholarly defenses of Germany decreased in number and depth of loyalty. Hostilities on the open seas and German espionage within America drove public sentiment increasingly toward intervention on the side of the Allies. Even respectable German attempts to win American sympathy, if not support, turned sour. German representatives formed the University League for American alumni of German schools, hoping that former students would produce a friendlier American attitude toward Germany. The University League had little success and many American scholars regarded it with scorn. A. B. Hart recalled the pressure placed on him to join "because I was known to be a Ph.D. of a German University, and they wanted to win over such people." He refused membership, referring to the group as just another of the German "secret agencies" for subverting America's position.[16] George B. Adams closed all avenues for a

---

[13] Schmitt, letter to editor, *Nation* 99 (24 August 1914): 251-52.

[14] Dodd to wife, 25 August 1914, quoted in Carol S. Gruber, "Mars and Minerva: World War One and the American Academic Man" (Ph.D. dissertation, Columbia University, 1968), p. 36.

[15] See John Burgess, *European War of 1914: Its Causes, Purposes and Probable Results* (Chicago, 1915); idem, *America's Relations to the Great War* (Chicago, 1916).

[16] A. B. Hart, "The Trail of the German: From the Reminiscences of Albert

German rapprochement when he told 500 wildly cheering Yale men in March 1917 that "we stand in a shameful place when we stand aloof," for if England should fall, "the doom of the United States is sounded."[17] While Chicago's Andrew C. McLaughlin might have agreed with this Anglophilism, he still feared the intolerance and extremism that would come with American entry. He asserted that war "arouses Prussianism in every nation; you cannot carry it on with silk gloves; the iron fisted come to the top."[18] The conflicts and qualms over America's position became a secondary issue when the declaration of war came in April 1917, but the question of the scholar's commitment to that war remained unanswered. Now with America at war, the problems of national unity, loyalty, service, and academic ethics all entered into the dilemma facing historians.

Less interested in the state of the academic world than in the state of loyalty in the Old Northwest, Claude H. Van Tyne had held an unequivocal position on the war since 1914. As chairman of the history department at the University of Michigan, he was sensitive about disloyalty among the large German-American population in his region, and as author of *The Loyalists in the American Revolution* he was prone to draw historical parallels for public enlightenment. In an indignant letter to the *New York Times* regarding Senator Robert LaFollette's opposition to the war, he lamented that "in the whole history of the United States, . . . I know of none but Aaron Burr who seems to me to have been more ready to betray democracy for his own selfish ends than the little Badger Napoleon, the Senator from Wisconsin."[19] Van Tyne had never been one to mince words or actions. Whether baiting his professors while a student in Heidelberg and Leipzig or cycling over the Rocky Mountains, his stance was aggressive, prompting one of his Michigan colleagues to comment that he was "vehement in pressing his own opinions and rather inclined to

---

Bushnell Hart," typed manuscript, 20 December 1918, p. 3, Hart Papers, New York Public Library.

[17] *New York Times*, 10 March 1917, p. 2.

[18] McLaughlin to Claude H. Van Tyne, 8 March 1917, Box 1, Van Tyne Papers, Michigan Historical Collection, Rackham Building, University of Michigan.

[19] *New York Times*, 21 August 1917, p. 8.

be intolerant of those whose standards differed from his."[20] For at least two years he had kept a stream of correspondence going to newspapers concerning the woeful state of military preparedness and his intentions of voting for Charles Evans Hughes in the presidential election of 1916 because Wilson had dealt so weakly with German outrages on American neutrality.[21] The declaration of war came none too soon for Van Tyne.

In the same spirit William Roscoe Thayer of Harvard had been ready for war long before America's entry. The author of studies of Cavour and John Hay, Thayer had written a book in 1916 called *Germany vs. Civilization* which he admitted was a "philippic."[22] The book displayed a polemical style and acute Germanophobia, indicating that Thayer favored relaxing some canons of historical objectivity during the war crisis. Thayer was to produce more than a dozen anti-German articles and books during the war, each exemplifying his militarist convictions. This same attitude revealed itself in public addresses in which he reduced issues to alternatives. Shortly before America's entry he originated the rather unabashed aphorism that "only a moral eunuch can be neutral," and during the war it became a much quoted phrase.[23]

Just as adamant as Van Tyne and Thayer in his sympathy for a vigorous war against Germany was Charles A. Beard of Columbia, who entertained an equally strong aversion to rampant nationalism. Beard's ambivalence was not an indication of doubt or timidity; his *Economic Interpretation of the Constitution* in 1913 had made him a figure of controversy and as early as the *Lusitania* crisis of 1915 he had declared himself at a faculty gathering as "quite strongly for intervention."[24] His defense of free speech, however, led him to suggest that the opinions of war opponents

20 Arthur L. Cross, "Claude H. Van Tyne," *Dictionary of American Biography*, rev. ed. (New York, 1936), 19: 217.

21 *New York Times*, 23 September 1915, p. 12, and 20 October 1916, p. 8.

22 Thayer to Mrs. Michael Foster, 6 March 1916, in Charles D. Hazen, ed., *The Letters of William Roscoe Thayer* (Boston, 1926), p. 277.

23 William Roscoe Thayer, *Volleys from a Non-Combatant* (Garden City, N. Y., 1919), p. 48. This speech was delivered in January 1917.

24 Quoted in James T. Shotwell, "Reminiscences," Columbia Oral History Collection, Columbia University, pp. 65-66.

"could not be changed by curses or bludgeons. Arguments addressed to their reason and understanding are our best hope."[25] This caution and respect for divergent views reflected a dispassionate approach that, ideally, trained historians were supposed to possess during peace or war, and compelled him to resign from the Columbia faculty late in 1917 in a well-publicized imbroglio concerning academic freedom.

Beard's Columbia colleague, James T. Shotwell, shared this sense of reserve. He, Beard, and James Harvey Robinson were close friends and shared neighboring offices on the Morningside Heights campus. They called themselves the Three Musketeers but still had many friendly disagreements on the world situation. Shotwell recalled that not until December 1916 did he finally join Beard in the conclusion "that the United States for its own sake, not just as an ally for the sake of the others, should enter the war to cast the balance against Germany."[26] He also shared with his colleague the fear of the excesses that war spirit could bring to the nation and to the historical profession. Writing to another historian of less restrained attitude, he expressed the hope that "we will be able to keep our sanity and deal with questions of fact" so that professors would not bring disrepute upon the academic world.[27]

Whether historians agreed with the aggressiveness of Van Tyne and Thayer or with the restraint of Beard and Shotwell, the choice was more of style than of substance. Historians generally agreed that they should be contributing to the war effort. One historian caught up in Wilson's crusading idealism later wrote, "We were only professors, but the world was still young, and we wanted to do something to beat the Hun and make the world safe for democracy."[28] Many felt that to continue their academic duties would not suffice. James G. Randall took leave from Roanoke College to join the United States Shipping Board. Ulrich B. Phillips left his post at the University of Michigan to become education secretary for the YMCA at Camp Gordon in

25 *New York Times*, 9 October 1917, p. 1.
26 Shotwell, "Reminiscences," pp. 66-67.
27 Shotwell to C. H. Van Tyne, 5 April 1917, Box 1, Van Tyne Papers.
28 Carl L. Becker, "La Belle France," *New Republic* 23 (14 July 1920): 207.

Georgia and found the work to be "the most inspiring thing I have ever experienced."[29]

Most historians did not experience the gratification that Phillips expressed with his war work. Some, such as the energetic but partly blind Thayer, regretted their inability to enter military service and had to content themselves with lecturing and writing. "In my Jack Horner way," Thayer mused, "I keep on issuing propaganda—firing arrows into the air at night—and quite ignorant of their effect. But this is all that is left to me now."[30] The same feeling of individual "uselessness" appears in the correspondence of Minnesota's Carl L. Becker and Harvard's Charles H. Haskins; they were too old for military duty and their talents were not being used elsewhere.[31] A nervous disorder rather than age kept William E. Dodd from joining the military and he grieved about "the injustice of staying at home when others give their lives for my safety."[32] Despite valuable work by some individual historians the majority were at a loss to make use of their "sound information."

Here then was an unmobilized army of scholars, ready to enlist their talents to justify America's part in the war, delineate historic causes of the struggle, and unify public opinion. As historians they seemed suited for the task of defining war issues and clarifying problems of nationalism, diplomacy, and commercial rivalries. They appeared ready to accept Emerson's exhortation to the American Scholar "to cheer, to raise, and to guide men by showing them facts amidst appearance." Wilson had appealed to their patriotic idealism and Jameson had appealed to their scholarly services; in order to respond effectively to these challenges they needed some form of organization through which they could channel their enthusiasm. Within days of America's entry into the war three major organizations would emerge to mobilize

[29] Phillips to C. H. Van Tyne, 4 November 1917, Box 1, Van Tyne Papers.

[30] Thayer to Charles F. Thwing, 15 April 1918, in Hazen, *Letters of W. R. Thayer*, p. 327.

[31] Haskins to C. L. Becker, 5 May 1917, Carl L. Becker Papers, Collection of Regional History, John M. Olin Research Library, Cornell University.

[32] Diary entry for 29 December 1917, in W. Alexander Mabry, ed., *Professor William E. Dodd's Diary, 1916-1920*, John P. Branch Historical Papers of Randolph-Macon College (Ashland, Va., 1953), pp. 55-56.

historians and offer them almost unlimited opportunities for war service. Once coordinated, these scholars would face the obvious problem of being at the same time historians and propagandists. Could the gap between the two be bridged or would the young community of scholars which prided itself on its professionalism succumb to the patriotic polemics that characterized its amateur predecessors? Generations of European scholars had faced this choice before and many of them had served with dubious honor as "court historians," offering intellectual buttressing for their nation's policies. Andrew C. McLaughlin set out the problem well and indicated his optimism when he wrote, "Perhaps few of us are able entirely to disentangle our scientific historical fibres from our swelling patriotic muscles, but most of us can try."[33]

[33] McLaughlin, "Historians in the War," *Dial* 62 (17 May 1917): 428.

II. Mobilizing the Historians

In his lofty Morningside Heights office, Professor James T. Shotwell assumed a somewhat Olympian position of anticipating events and serving as a catalyst for their implementation. He and Charles A. Beard had urged America's entry into the war months before Wilson's address, and now in early April Shotwell became a leader in organizing historians for war activity. What now began as a series of talks and letters grew into the National Board for Historical Service, one of three major committees in which historians participated during the war. Following a meeting with his Columbia colleagues at the time of the war message, Shotwell related that they found "when it came to positive action there did not seem to be any particular place for our services" other than contributing to a series of faculty pamphlets and encouraging the university library to collect and coordinate war materials. He wrote several friends about the problem of undirected historical talent and asked if they thought "it would be a good thing for the History men from the various universities to form a little Joint Committee to consider the problem as a whole."[1]

These preliminary probes found receptive subjects and soon Frederick Jackson Turner (now of Harvard) and J. Franklin Jameson joined Shotwell's recruitment crusade. The three invited several other historians to a conference to be held in Washington on April 28 "respecting what History men can do for their country now." The invitation pointed out the need for coordination; many historians "would doubtless be glad to spend a good deal of time in public service in wartime, . . . but are not in the way of hearing of useful tasks that they could undertake."[2] Fifteen historians responded, crowded into Jameson's office in the Carnegie Institution, and adopted Andrew McLaughlin's attitude that they should cease being mere chroniclers of the past and should dare to use their talent and training for "prophecy and actual guidance."[3] Accordingly they established the National Board for Historical Service (NBHS), with headquarters in Washington, "to facilitate the coordination and development of Historical activities in the United States in such a way as to aid the Federal and the State governments. . . . To aid in supplying the public with trustworthy information of historical or similar character . . . through the giving of lectures and of systematic instruction and in other ways."[4]

The charter members of the Board paid tribute to Shotwell by electing him chairman, a choice both fitting and expedient; with his talent for organization and his many friends in the profession he could offer active leadership for historians. Only forty-two at the time, he had yet to establish himself as a prolific author, but his reputation as an editor and lecturer was solid. He had earned his doctorate at Columbia and had been teaching there since 1900 while also serving as assistant general editor of the *Encyclopaedia Britannica.* His popularity as a professor apparently came as much from his personal magnetism as from his academic credentials; his deep resonant voice, leonine head, and wavy hair contributed to a commanding presence which attracted friends and followers. One of his students during the war years remembered that in 1917 he was part of a retinue which "admired Shotwell more than any other historian."[5]

Although his Quaker background would have discouraged jingoism, Shotwell had by 1916 become convinced that America must aid in the defeat of Germany in order to maintain a workable balance of power and international peace. He accepted the NBHS chairmanship with enthusiasm and set out to impose his point of view on America which he feared "in spite of all that happened

[1] Shotwell to C. H. Van Tyne, 5 April 1917, Box 1, Van Tyne Papers, Michigan Historical Collection, Rackham Building, University of Michigan.

[2] Circular letter to Max Farrand, Charles Hazen, Andrew C. McLaughlin, and others, 20 April 1917, Box 25, National Board for Historical Service Records (hereafter cited as NBHS Records), Manuscript Division, Library of Congress.

[3] McLaughlin to Jameson, 25 April 1917, Box 63, File 1081, Jameson Papers, Manuscript Division, Library of Congress.

[4] Charter resolution adopted 29 April 1917, Box 25 NBHS Records.

[5] Harry Elmer Barnes to author, 13 April 1968.

in Europe in the three dreadful years previously was utterly unprepared."[6] Many observers attributed his enthusiasm to more
than just American patriotism; he had spent more than half
of his life in his native Canada and had completed his undergraduate training there in British-oriented schools. A few historians even entertained the prevalent but unsubstantiated theory
that his fervor in organizing war activities gained impetus from
financial remuneration by Britain and France.[7] Whether his
motives were primarily American, British, financial, or pacifist,
his actions as NBHS chairman were openly anti-German and aimed
at engaging as many historians as possible in the struggle.

Shotwell resigned the chair in November 1917 because of ill-
ness, but maintained a close relationship with the Board, suggesting projects and channeling historians into its activities throughout
the war. The NBHS leadership passed to an equally international
and more cautious personality, Evarts B. Greene. Born of American
missionary parents in Japan, Greene had studied at Northwestern
University, Berlin, and Harvard, where he received his doctorate
in 1893. At the time of the war he had spent his entire teaching
career at the University of Illinois and American historians recognized him as an authority in colonial and revolutionary fields.
A soft-spoken and somewhat absent-minded bachelor, Greene
brought a quiet leadership to the post that was less anti-German
and more idealistic than that of Shotwell. When he resigned in
September 1918 to direct Illinois's University War Committee,
Princeton's Dana C. Munro assumed the chairmanship until the
NBHS disbanded in December of the following year. Munro was
a widely-traveled historian, having studied in Strassburg and Freiburg, and taught at Pennsylvania and Wisconsin before settling
down in 1916 as chairman of Princeton's history department. A
charter member of the Board, he shared Greene's circumspect
attitude on war issues and Shotwell's diplomatic involvement,
an interest which directed many NBHS historians into the work of
the Inquiry, planning for the Versailles conference.

[6] James T. Shotwell, "Reminiscences," Columbia Oral History Collection,
Columbia University, p. 60.

[7] Harry Elmer Barnes to author, 13 April 1968.

Jameson's activity in the new NBHS assumed a less public character than did that of the three chairmen but it was no less important. One of the prime movers in its creation, Jameson became a member of the executive board and as managing editor of the *American Historical Review* gave the NBHS more publicity in its pages than the board could have acquired otherwise. Neither could the NBHS have undertaken the volume of work that it did without the assistance Jameson solicited from the Carnegie Institution. From this philanthropic and educational body he received sufficient free office space in Washington to house the historians' operations and also financial grants large enough to support the Board's clerical, traveling, printing, and mailing expenses.[8] His direct involvement in the Board programs provided a respectability that few others could have supplied and drew into service reluctant scholars who otherwise would have remained aloof. But perhaps his most significant contribution to the NBHS came through his editorial and research assistant, Waldo G. Leland.

Leland had studied under Jameson at Brown University before pursuing graduate work at Harvard and now assisted Jameson at both the *Review* and the Carnegie Institution. His work with manuscripts, bibliographies, and archivists had brought him into a kind of liaison position among professional and amateur historians. Not an academic historian himself, he nevertheless commanded the respect of other professionals and had been secretary of the American Historical Association since 1909. He was present at the birth of the NBHS and Jameson relieved him of some of the *Review* duties so that he might become secretary-treasurer of the new group. Until the Board terminated in December 1919, Leland was often its major, albeit anonymous, stabilizing force. During its thirty-two month existence, while the executive board expanded from nine to twenty-five and the chairmanship changed hands twice, Leland remained one of the few charter members whose executive tenure spanned the life of the Board. His longevity became doubly important as a unifying element because the Board held formal meetings only five times, most of its activity being

8 Jameson to F. J. Turner, 13 June 1917, Box 85, File 1653, Jameson Papers.

carried out by smaller subcommittees operating independently of each other. In his liaison position Leland coordinated these disparate activities, solicited funds from businessmen to finance particularly ambitious tasks, and found summer school and semester replacements for historians undertaking off-campus NBHS projects. His final accomplishment was a logical manifestation of his ubiquitous role, that of collecting the records of the NBHS and providing the only comprehensive written account of its work.[9]

Within two days of the NBHS's inauguration a nationwide network of correspondence began to connect it with individual historians in scores of colleges and universities. The Board circulated a letter on May 1 announcing its existence to 165 historians whose names Leland had compiled from his familiar *Review* mailing list. The letter explained the voluntary and unofficial status of the Board and how it hoped to use historical talent for mass education. It inquired about projects and individuals who would donate services, and in general invited historians to join a kind of *ad hoc* patriotic union.[10] The letter drew a heavy response in favor of the Board but some historians expressed reservations about the still amorphous plans. E. D. Adams wrote from Stanford University that "the impression it makes upon me is that of a group of historians at Washington, very anxious to do something for their country and plunging, without sufficient consideration into this movement, which may perhaps embarrass more than it will help our national cause."[11] Subsequent correspondence from the Board attempted to counter such reservations and offered more definite suggestions for helpful historical projects. Turner proposed that professors make their classes and research seminars more relevant to war issues, and Leland outlined several opportunities in another circular letter which went to an expanded mailing list of 225. He suggested lecturing before schools, churches, and clubs, writing articles for newspapers and magazines, and developing special courses in school systems.[12]

[9] Leland, "National Board for Historical Service," in Newton D. Mereness, ed., *American Historical Activities during the World War: Annual Report of the American Historical Association, 1919* (Washington, D. C., 1923), 1: 161-89.
[10] Box 25, NBHS Records.
[11] Adams to W. G. Leland, 16 May 1917, Box 1, NBHS Records.
[12] Circular letters, 11 and 13 May 1917, Box 25, NBHS Records.

At the end of the Board's formative month Jameson reflected on its growth and its crystallizing plans. "I believe that much good will come from the movement and that many history-men, eager to serve the country, but not seeing precisely how, will by these means find an opportunity to be useful."[13] His belief materialized. The NBHS gained clearer purposes during the war and undertook tasks of more than temporary interest. In pamphleteering, arranging speaking tours, revising school curricula, and investigating government projects it offered historians opportunities to channel their activities into organized propaganda work. Even the editors of the *Mississippi Valley Historical Review* seemed impressed and relaxed their strictures regarding historians and war work. In 1914 they had looked with disdain upon historians who became purveyors of wartime nationalism; now in June 1917 one of them encouraged historians to take advantage of the NBHS programs.[14]

The Committee on Public Information (CPI) was created a few days before the NBHS was established but was slower in developing projects for historians. Rather than impose government censorship on the American press, President Wilson created the CPI on April 13, 1917, as a clearinghouse for war information. He appointed four directors: Secretary of State Robert Lansing, Secretary of War Newton D. Baker, Secretary of the Navy Josephus Daniels, and George Creel, a professional journalist who had campaigned for progressive reform and for Wilson's reelection in 1916. The major initiative and administration of the committee belonged to only one of these men; as Baker later evaluated the four directors, "while our names have been used as members of the Committee on Public Information, its labors have been the labors of Mr. Creel."[15]

Under Creel's leadership the CPI grew into a spectacular propaganda mechanism, publicizing American war aims and ideals at home and abroad and setting countless precedents for government

[13] Jameson to Frank A. Golder, 23 May 1917 (copy), Box 92, Jameson Papers.

[14] *Mississippi Valley Historical Review* (hereafter cited as MVHR) 1 (December 1914): 481; 4 (June 1917): 140.

[15] Newton D. Baker, Introduction to George Creel, *How We Advertised America* (New York, 1920), p. xi.

manipulation of public opinion. Never before had there been a federal agency for the express purpose of manufacturing and distributing ideas. While much of the American war effort still bore the imprint of the nineteenth century, the CPI was a true child of the twentieth, using modern methods of psychology, mass production, and advertising to market its product. The story of the famous Four Minute Men orators, Charles Dana Gibson's army of poster artists, the mobilization of Hollywood's film producers, and the legion of businessmen and academicians who campaigned for Wilsonian idealism in foreign countries still offers instructive reading. Of the twenty-one subcommittees within the CPI—each aiming its barrage of words or pictures in a different direction—perhaps the least spectacular was the Division of Civic and Educational Cooperation, a committee made up almost exclusively of historians.

Despite his lack of training as a scholar, Creel deserves credit for creating this committee of historians and appointing a director who could, it was hoped, straddle the chasm which separated propaganda from professional history. Realizing his own inability to "reach the people through their minds, rather than through their emotions," Creel sought someone who could supervise a publicity campaign aimed at a higher level than most of the work being done by the CPI. What he said he needed was "a university man, the practised historian, the writer skilled in investigation, one who knew America and Europe equally well. It was at this moment that there came into my hands a pamphlet containing a patriotic address given out in Minnesota by one Guy Stanton Ford. I have rarely read anything that made a more instant impression, for it had beauty without sacrifice of force, simplicity, remarkable sequence, and obvious knowledge."[16] On investigation Creel found that Ford was chairman of the history department and dean of the graduate school at the University of Minnesota as well as the author of several works on German history,[17] all of which seemed to qualify him for the work Creel

---

[16] Creel, *How We Advertised America*, pp. 100-101.

[17] See Ford, *Hanover and Prussia, 1795-1803* (New York, 1903); idem, "Boyen's Military Law," *AHR* 20 (April 1915): 528-38.

had in mind. With a flurry of telegrams between Washington and Minnesota, Creel invited Ford into government service, NBHS chairman Shotwell urged him to accept the invitation, and Ford consented to be "drafted" as director of the Division of Civic and Educational Cooperation.[18]

Ford was a product of American historical training and many phases of his career had overlapped that of his friend Shotwell. A son of the Wisconsin middle border, he had done undergraduate work at Madison under Turner before receiving his doctorate at Columbia in 1903, the same year as Shotwell. His commitment to the war had come at roughly the same time as his friend's and during his 1916 sabbatical he participated in Plattsburg's military training program, becoming a drill master when he returned to the Minnesota campus. He gave immediate support to the NBHS as a charter member and later speculated that Shotwell had probably alerted Creel to the pamphlet which led to his appointment as coordinator of historical activities within the CPI.[19] In his mid-forties he appeared to be more a contemporary of Jameson, who was nearly sixty, probably because his graying hair, his stern, spectacled visage, and his position as dean of a graduate school created an impression of age and authority.

When Ford came to Washington he found that his new division consisted of himself and several undeveloped ideas that swirled around in the chaos of the infant CPI. Creel trusted him implicitly and granted him a free hand in developing programs, recruiting other historians, and using government facilities. In his office in an old residence unoccupied since the days of Andrew Jackson, Ford found upon arrival no desks or typewriters but an abundance of painters, carpenters, and newspapermen.[20] One of these journalists described the same scene a few months later when Ford's division had increased its personnel and developed many of its

[18] Creel to Ford, 8 May 1917 (copy); Shotwell to Ford, 8 May 1917 (copy); Ford to Creel, 9 May 1917—all in Committee on Public Information Records, National Archives, Record Group 63 (hereafter cited as CPI Records), 3-A1, Tray 1.

[19] Guy Stanton Ford, "Reminiscences," Columbia Oral History Collection, copy at the University of Minnesota Library, 2: 369-71.

[20] Ford, "America's Fight for Public Opinion," *Minnesota History Bulletin* 3 (February 1919): 11.

ideas. It was all "in one room—one room and a half, to be exact. It is one director, one assistant, one stenographer, two desks—and the best historical talent in America."[21]

Samuel B. Harding occupied the second desk in Ford's office and supplied much of the historical talent for the CPI. A Hoosier with a Harvard Ph.D., Harding had taught European history at Indiana University since 1895 and had been a member with Ford on the executive council of the American Historical Association as well as the NBHS. Ford would have been hard-pressed to find an assistant with a more varied or colorful background. In addition to publishing European history textbooks and classroom maps, Harding had written with his wife a series of popular children's books on ancient history. Harding came from a family with newspaper and publishing interests and he still carried his type-setters' membership card. This background proved invaluable when the division began publishing its war literature. According to Ford, "He knew all about it. I would just simply turn the question over to him . . . and pretty soon he would have those fresh, modern fellows backed off the boards completely, because he knew more about make-up, arrangements of printing material and all that kind of thing than they ever dreamed of."[22]

From their cramped room and a half, Ford and Harding encouraged their history colleagues to work on projects for the CPI at their respective campuses, calling them to Washington only on rare occasions. Ford had taught at Yale and Illinois before his tenure at Minnesota and his wide-spread circle of friends became potential CPI aides. Likewise, he and Harding found their membership in the NBHS a great help in getting other historians to offer their services. Ford later recalled at a congressional hearing that of all groups which offered to assist his division, the NBHS had done the most.[23] The close affiliation of these two organizations was mutually advantageous. Leland pointed out that the

---

[21] Donald Wilhelm, "The Government's Own Publicity Work," *Review of Reviews* 56 (November 1917): 510.

[22] Ford, "Reminiscences," 2: 376.

[23] U. S., Congress, House, *Sundry Civil Bill, 1919: Hearings before Subcommittee of House Committee on Appropriations*, part 3, *Committee on Public Information*, 65 Cong., 2 sess. (Washington, D. C., 1918), pp. 101-2.

appointment of Ford to the CPI was the best thing that could have happened to the NBHS, for it gave the latter organization official government contacts and leverage for its own work.[24]

Drawing on the resources of the United States government and the talent of his colleagues, Ford faced the problem of satisfying the demands of an official "line" while remaining faithful to his profession. The threat of becoming a court historian who interprets history to suit the demands of an employer was an obvious danger; equally dangerous was the problem of allowing a divided and unenlightened nation to fall victim of all manner of "unsound" historical information from less scrupulous sources. Most of Ford's friends were sure he would be able to maintain his intellectual independence despite being a government employee. Leland was still convinced four months later that Ford had not been forced to shift his attitude to conform with CPI directives. He wrote Jameson that Ford "is having his own way about the work of the committee" and was formulating his own program unrestricted by his superiors.[25] Others remained skeptical. The CPI was an unprecedented organization in American history with extraordinary influence over the coordination and distribution of government information. Because of this newness and its quick assumption of power, the CPI aroused suspicion and distrust and many feared it, unjustly as it turned out, as an agent of government intimidation and censorship. Wilson placed the CPI under the jurisdiction of the Executive Department to be funded from presidential appropriations; this act alone symbolized the intellectual and financial control he could wield over historians within the committee. Many congressmen suspected the CPI of being a presidential mouthpiece, and during the second year of the war Wilson reluctantly transferred financial control of the committee to Congress, which promptly cut its budget and publicly chastized some of its operations. The presence of the rambunctious George Creel as CPI director did not make the historians' lot any easier. His talent for sensational journalism and for creating enemies

24 Leland to Evarts B. Greene, 5 September 1917, Box 3, NBHS Records.

25 W. G. Leland to J. F. Jameson, 2 September 1917, Box 58, File 987, Jameson Papers.

was well known. Mark Sullivan reflected that "where ever he was, in whatever public role, trouble, commotion, angry controversy arose about him as surely as smoke goes upward."[26] The situation for historians, therefore, was at best precarious. They served three masters: Wilson, Congress, and Creel, all of whom differed slightly on important issues.

Ford naturally remained noncommittal about the dilemma. He outlined the problem before congressmen but offered no solution. "In the beginning it was not quite clear how we were going to do this. . . . It is absolutely unbroken ground, for which we had no precedent. . . . This work has grown up and grown up very accidentally, one might say, and the work came first and the methods came afterwards."[27] Accidentally or by design, court history or not, the work of the Ford division, subsidized by the federal government, was monumental in scope. Several dozen historians enrolled in its ranks to become pamphleteers, speakers, investigators, catalogers, editors and school curricula revisers. Under the CPI aegis, their work reached a wider audience than the propaganda of any independent agency operating during the war, and like many other federal war activities ended abruptly with the armistice.

While the CPI and the NBHS cooperated closely and benefitted from government facilities, a third organization, the National Security League (NSL), waged a separate but related educational battle. Chartered in January 1915 as a corporation in New York state, the NSL outlined its purpose to "promote education and national sentiment and service among the people of the United States and to promote recognition of the fact that the obligation of universal military service requires universal military training."[28] This emphasis on military preparedness reflected the sentiments of the League's founder, S. Stanwood Menken, a New York corporation lawyer who had been on a European business trip when war broke out in August 1914. Temporarily stranded in

[26] Sullivan, *Over Here, 1914-1918*, vol. 5 in *Our Times: The United States, 1900-1925*, 6 vols. (New York, 1926-1935), p. 426.

[27] U. S., Congress, *Hearings, Sundry Civil Bill, 1919*, part 3, p. 95.

[28] NSL Charter, reprinted in U. S., *Congressional Record*, 65 Cong., 3 sess., p. 5063.

England, he occupied part of his time by sitting in the visitors' gallery of the House of Commons, listening to debates on a war revenue bill. Menken later recalled that he was aghast at the lack of English readiness for war and he feared that "the United States was wholly unprepared to meet a similar catastrophe."[29] When he returned home he conferred with several like-minded men, such as Theodore Roosevelt and his former secretary of war, Henry L. Stimson, General Leonard Wood, George Haven Putnam, the Anglophilic publisher, and Massachusetts Representative Augustus P. Gardner, who was Henry Cabot Lodge's son-in-law. They agreed that the threat to American security demanded larger military appropriations and that the best way to achieve this would be by arousing public opinion to convince the federal government of the need. From these talks came the formation of the NSL with Menken as its first president and many well known figures, such as Elihu Root and Alton B. Parker, conspicuously advertised as honorary officers to gain more attention.[30]

Until American entry in the war made its preparedness campaign obsolete, the League lobbied for compulsory military training and larger congressional naval and armaments appropriations, and engaged in various crusades to gain popular support. NSL speakers traveled across the country scaring local chambers of commerce, Rotary and Kiwanis groups, and schools with speculations on the imminent collapse of the Allies and on German invasions of the United States. These techniques won many converts and the NSL soon had branch organizations in twenty-two states and a membership estimated as high as 100,000. Menken's business and political acquaintances underwrote much of the financial burden, but he could still boast of contributions from thousands of patriotic citizens, "mostly in $1 bills."[31] With this backing the League supported the Plattsburg training camp program, opposed antiwar politicians, and organized massive preparedness parades to pressure Wilson into a more aggressive stance.

[29] Quoted in editorial, "National Security League," *Outlook* 112 (16 February 1916): 351.

[30] The only scholarly survey of the NSL is Robert D. Ward, "The Origin and Activities of the National Security League, 1914-1919," *MVHR* 47 (June 1960): 51-65.

[31] *New York Times*, 14 March 1917, p. 2.

America's declaration of war changed the League's emphasis but did not lessen its fervor. Preparedness campaigns gave way to loyalty crusades, Americanization programs for immigrant groups, and civic education in schools. The NSL leadership became increasingly conservative as businessmen began to replace political and military figures, and by the end of the war critics of the League accused it of being a Republican lobby group. After the armistice the League declined sharply, unable to sustain public support for military programs, and it devoted its final days to fighting socialism and communism. Before the ideological transformation occurred, however, the NSL was one of the more effective groups in mobilizing support for the war effort, particularly with the work of one of its subcommittees—the Committee on Patriotism Through Education. Historians dominated this group, and two of them, A. B. Hart and Princeton's Robert M. McElroy, generated more publicity for the League than any of its other varied personnel.

Hart infused his NSL work with the same energetic and outspoken qualities that characterized his personality and professional career. He had begun teaching at Harvard in 1883 after receiving his Ph.D. at Germany's Freiburg University and had remained at his undergraduate alma mater ever since. A prolific writer and editor with ambitious hopes for America's historical profession, he was instrumental in establishing the *American Historical Review* and became widely known and respected for editing the *American Nation* series. Both the American Historical Association and the American Political Science Association had honored him with their presidential offices and three decades of Harvard students knew him affectionately as "Bushy," a name derived from his middle name, Bushnell, and also from his flamboyant handlebar moustache and beard. Hart's contempt for Germany grew as the war lengthened and he enjoyed denigrating for his students the supposed superiority of German universities. He frequently told of how he had caught the priggish professor Treitschke making errors in his lectures, that there were no longer any "eminent professors of history in Germany," and that the only thing now worth partaking of in Germany was beer.[32]

[32] Hart testimony in U. S., Congress, Senate, *Brewing and Liquor Interests and*

Hart commanded an audience well beyond academic circles. His friendship with Theodore Roosevelt and editors of the *New York Times* afforded him opportunities to expound on national and international events, opportunities which he seemed to relish and seldom refused. From his office in Widener Library came a stream of articles and books advocating Republican programs, firm foreign policy, and military preparedness. One of his Harvard acquaintances remembered him as a "super-patriot" whose Roose-veltian partisanship led him to accuse President Wilson of coward-ice for his timidity with Germany before the war declaration.[33] He had been less doctrinaire about America's position than his colleague Thayer, but no less outspoken. As featured speakers at the Congress of Constructive Patriotism in Washington's DAR Hall in January 1917, he and Thayer presented forceful arguments for League goals of civic education, national readiness, and com-pulsory military training. It was at this gathering that Thayer first branded neutrals as "moral eunuchs," prompting one journalist to refer to the speakers as "American Virility in Convention As-sembled."[34] Ironically, when war came Hart admitted that beneath his militant rhetoric "I freely own that I feel scared, not about the Germans but about being waked up ourselves."[35]

With a call for readiness, Hart sought out other historians as speakers to inform the nation about the causes of the war and needs for defense and victory. His organizing efforts produced the Speakers Training Camp held at Chautauqua in July 1917. Designed to coincide with Independence Day festivities, this meeting was billed as one to "inform and arouse" because "the country sorely needs clear, definite, authentic information of the situation of the world and our own position as a belligerent power. It equally needs to be aroused to the absolute necessity of organiz-ing our men, materials and government in such a way to meet

---

German Propaganda: Hearings before a Subcommittee on the Judiciary, 65 Cong., 2 and 3 sess. (Washington, D. C., 1919), 2: 1622-23.

[33] Richard A. Newhall to author, 7 April 1968.

[34] NSL, *Proceedings of the Congress of Constructive Patriotism* (New York, 1917), pp. 278-85; Frederick M. Davenport, "American Virility in Convention Assembled," *Outlook* 115 (7 February 1917): 227-29.

[35] Hart to W. G. Leland, 8 May 1917, Box 3, NBHS Records.

the terrifically concentrated force of our great enemy, Germany."[36] One of Hart's speakers failed to turn up and Robert McElroy substituted on short notice. Hart was impressed with his work during the Chautauqua sessions and soon had him working with the League. Later that year when Hart retired as chairman, McElroy assumed the leadership of the Committee on Patriotism Through Education.

McElroy brought to his work the same emotional fervor and commitment to the war that Hart had displayed. If he was considerably younger and less well known than his Harvard associate, his aggressiveness and theatrical presence made an immediate impact on the League. He had studied in Germany for a year after receiving his doctorate at Princeton in 1900, then returned to accept a position in the history department, becoming chairman shortly after Woodrow Wilson departed for the New Jersey governor's office. Born near a Civil War battlefield in Kentucky, his martial spirit found an outlet in the early days of the Plattsburg program and in instituting military drills on his own campus. He had been out of the country the year preceding America's entry into war and had just returned from Tsing Hua College in China, eager to get involved in the war, when Hart asked him to serve with the NSL. Handsome, well-built, and a youthful forty-five, McElroy cut a striking figure in his dapper pin-stripe suits with a silver pin in his lapel, emblazoned with the NSL crest.

McElroy soon became educational director for the entire League but his duties remained similar to those established by Hart— organizing other historians to combat apathy and misconceptions about America's role in the war.[37] He dramatized his work with a verve reminiscent of the July 4 atmosphere in which he first encountered the League, and attacked enemies on the homefront as if they were German trenches in France. His task entailed many of the same projects undertaken by both the CPI and the NBHS:

[36] Circular letter, 3 May 1917, Box 12, William E. Dodd Papers, Manuscript Division, Library of Congress; A. B. Hart, *Reasons for and Objects of Speakers Training Camp for Education in Patriotic Service and Conference of Organizations Engaged in Patriotic Education* (New York, 1917), p. 6.
[37] Although McElroy assumed Hart's NSL position, Hart remained active and worked closely with McElroy throughout the war.

pamphleteering, arranging speaking tours, helping revise school curricula, and investigating disloyal activities and literature. Considering the militant and sprightly leadership, it is little wonder that historians who participated in the programs of the NSL found their work both lively and controversial.[38]

When the initial flag-waving and patriotic organizing had given way to the day-to-day process of educating America, many historians began to experience misgivings. Some feared that the flush of nationalism would cause historians to lose their individual balance once caught up in group activity. They feared their voluntary mobilization might become regimentation and their historical training might be exploited to sanction doctrines not of their own conscience. Members of the NBHS, CPI, and NSL all voiced these misgivings; none of the three groups possessed a monopoly of self-confidence. John Latane, a diplomatic historian at Johns Hopkins working with the NSL, wrote that he feared the reaction of some overly patriotic organizations might be to "lose all historical perspective and to assume extreme and untenable positions."[39] Another professor was dubious about the effects of mobilization on scholarship and urged the CPI to "stand by all the rules of historical method."[40] Some of the more conservative historians suspected that patriotic service was just another means by such progressives as Beard and Shotwell to impose the New History on the profession. They had rejected before the war this philosophy of "using" the past as an aid for bringing about social reform and did not want to see it adopted by another name during the national crisis.

European scholars who had recently capitulated to the passions of nationalism and war gave justification to these fears of group activity. Ninety-three German scholars had earned widespread contempt late in 1914 when they signed the infamous manifesto which defended German actions and denied responsibility for

[38] Fewer historians joined the NSL projects than those sponsored by the CPI and NBHS, but their activity generally received more publicity.

[39] Latane to F. J. Turner, 15 June 1917, Box 4, NBHS Records.

[40] Edward Krehbiel (Stanford) to G. S. Ford, 24 September 1917, 3-Al, Tray 24, CPI Records.

perpetrating the crisis. The signatories included several noted German historians, a fact that prompted James Harvey Robinson to describe the episode as "the sign and seal of the success of German *Kultur* in making all her subjects accept the Kaiser and his decisions."[41] Even the Allies were not immune to the herd instinct of war. Jameson lamented that French historians were turning the respected *Revue Historique* into a journal of self-serving chauvinism.[42] Turner seemed to synthesize these qualms when he reported that "the attitude of the men as a whole I should say is (what is natural to all scholars) that history and *ex parte* propaganda will be mixed."[43]

No matter how zealously they tried to mask and modify the word, it rankled. Propaganda and historians! Could the contradiction of terms be resolved or would the collective efforts of historians—regardless of how well meant—remain a mark on their reputations? Perhaps in deference to Ford's division, Creel tried to sidestep the issue. "We did not call it 'propaganda,' for that word, in German hands, had come to be associated with lies and corruption. Our work was educational and informative."[44] The NSL did not quibble. President Menken instructed his scholars to rouse and shock the American public into patriotic action.[45] Part of their sensitivity to the term doubtless came from the propaganda that the Allied and Central Powers had disseminated in America since 1914. Inundated with pamphlets from the belligerents—the red, yellow, blue, and white books of documents proclaiming their respective guilt or innocence for the war—Americans came to realize that editing could produce a case for any argument. The British Bryce Report of atrocities in Belgium and the capture of a German agent's portfolio of espionage in America further revealed that truth had become a salable commodity.

As a scholar and politician President Wilson offered leadership

[41] Robinson, "War and Thinking," *New Republic* 1 (19 December 1914): 17-18.
[42] Jameson to C. L. Becker, 2 May 1917, Becker Papers, Collection of Regional History, John M. Olin Research Library, Cornell University.
[43] F. J. Turner to Jameson, 20 May 1917, Box 85, File 1653, Jameson Papers.
[44] U. S., *Complete Report of the Chairman of the Committee on Public Information, 1917-1918-1919* (Washington, D. C., 1920), p. 1 (hereafter cited as CPI, *Complete Report*).
[45] National Security League, *Annual Meeting, 1917* (New York, 1917), p. 6.

for historians that was at once real and symbolic. One pro-German journalist even labeled him the High Priest of Propaganda.[46] He created the CPI himself and many of the men joining the three organizations had been his professors, students, and academic associates. With his crusading zeal he raised the nation to a novel peak of patriotic service. The postwar disenchantment which replaced Wilsonian idealism parallels the reappraisals which greeted historians who followed his leadership and incorporated his idealism into their war work. Historians who joined the CPI, NBHS, and NSL neither constituted a majority of the profession nor claimed to be spokesmen for it. With few exceptions they were luminaries in the academic field and therefore not typical. Their activity as propagandists was unprecedented, widely publicized, and, because of their stature in the profession, erroneously regarded as representative of American historical thinking. As showpieces rather than spokesmen they offered only symbolic leadership for their colleagues, but they brought very real repercussions to their scholarly guild.

[46] George Sylvester Viereck, *Spreading Germs of Hate* (New York, 1930), p. 168. Viereck was one of the most active propagandists for the German cause and edited *The Fatherland* in New York.

III. Professors & Pamphlets

When *The War Message and the Facts behind It* came off the Government Printing Office presses on June 10, 1917, historians in the CPI and NBHS became official pamphleteers. Unsure whether their efforts were properly aimed, they had ordered only 20,000 copies of this initial pamphlet and hoped their work would find an audience. They need not have worried. Director Ford later recalled that "as soon as it was released and the newspapers noticed it, the first day after that I got a peach basket full of mail . . . and the next day two bushels, and then the flood just opened on us." By the end of the war, 2,499,903 copies were in circulation[1] and historians had established themselves and pamphleteering as effective agents of literary propaganda.

The CPI-NBHS pamphleteers repeated this effort more than thirty times during the war with varying success and produced a small monument of "popular history." One of the most sympathetic critics of their work was the Indiana author Booth Tarkington, who helped distribute many of the pamphlets in the Midwest. He wrote Ford about public opinion and the effects of propaganda among his Hoosier neighbors. "These people are avid and loyal, but not at all clear as to *what* we are fighting; somewhat mystified, too, as to why. Now and then a fisherman will say, 'Well, I *have* heard *some* tellin' around that it's a kind of a capitalist's war; dunno whether it's so or not.' Talk doesn't explain to him. . . . But if he reads a pamphlet 'got out by the United States Gov'ment' he is 'impressed!' "[2] As colloquial as *Penrod*, Tarkington's appraisal reinforced the CPI-NBHS historians in their belief that the pamphlets would find readers. Ford analyzed the situation shrewdly. "We did not have to make the demand. The demand was there."[3]

Meeting this demand proved one of the vexing problems for both the CPI and the NSL. The mere physical task of printing and distributing bulk material in an orderly fashion was one that neither organization resolved, although both received support from other agencies. During the war CPI-NBHS historians printed more than 33,000,000 of their pamphlets which were distributed by congressmen, YMCA's, chambers of commerce, Boy Scouts, school teachers, state defense councils, political parties, and the Departments of State and Agriculture.[4] Magazines reprinted many pamphlets and newspapers serialized some, making total readership impossible to estimate. Even with these volunteer helpers circulating the pamphlets, serious bottlenecks still prohibited a smooth distribution. The government presses could not meet the demand for the more popular items and often fell weeks behind on printing schedules, forcing the CPI to commission some of its work to private printers. Ford urged school principals to incorporate the pamphlets into their teaching programs and then found it difficult to meet the incoming orders. At one point he had to deny historians complimentary copies of their own pamphlets, so short was the supply.[5] The resulting stack of complaining correspondence was undoubtedly frustrating but not nearly so much so as a stack of unwanted pamphlets would have been.

The NSL kept fewer publication and circulation records than did the CPI but its methods and results were similar. McElroy cooperated with Ford to obtain franking privileges for occasional intensive mailing campaigns and the NBHS also helped advertise NSL pamphlets by recommending them to school administrators and teachers.[6] This casual cooperation among the three groups enhanced the prestige of League pamphlets, for if Tarkington's Indiana patriots were typical of average Americans, the more official a pamphlet appeared the more readily they accepted it. If for no other reason than this visual impact, many NSL pamphlets closely resembled the CPI format and bore the League crest, which

[1] U. S., Congress, House, *Sundry Civil Bill, 1919: Hearings before Subcommittee of House Committee on Appropriations*, part 3, *Committee on Public Information*, 65 Cong., 2 sess. (Washington, D. C., 1918), p. 96; CPI, *Complete Report*, p. 16.

[2] Tarkington to G. S. Ford, 19 December 1917, 3-A1, Tray 8, CPI Records.

[3] U. S., Congress, *Hearings, Sundry Civil Bill, 1919*, part 3, p. 96.

[4] Ibid., pp. 18-19.

[5] Ford to William Stearns Davis, n.d., 1917, Correspondence Folder, 1914-1917, Davis Papers, University of Minnesota Library.

[6] Oddly enough there was little if any criticism of this use of franking rights.

appeared, on first glance, to be some kind of government emblem.

Getting pamphlets into circulation was a large physical problem. Filling them with historically respectable propaganda was something else. Historians had long recognized the influential role of pamphlets in the history of propaganda. Ford acknowledged that Thomas Paine's *Common Sense* and *The Crisis* had been the CPI pamphlets of Revolutionary times.[7] Descendants of the Paine pamphlets, one may note, had appeared in almost every phase of American political history, from abolitionist appeals to feminist crusades, and had ranged from scholarly treatises on English constitutional law to scurrilous attacks on the Roman Catholic church. Cheap to produce and easy to digest, a pamphlet could offer a singular argument to a mass audience. McElroy's work as education director paid tribute to the pamphleteering techniques of selectivity, simplification, and speed, and NSL pamphlets concentrated on singular topics directed at reaching the American mind as quickly as possible.[8]

Emphasis on speed helped to distinguish NSL pamphlets from those produced by the CPI. McElroy, anxious to impart information by the "quickest possible method," often allowed or asked his historians to produce pamphlets without close supervision from NSL directors. Ford required each historian to submit his work to editorial scrutiny by several other historians, which often resulted in composite authorship. This group approach to pamphleteering did not deny credit to individual authors responsible for several CPI publications, but none of these appeared under the CPI imprint before receiving approval from Ford, government officials, and a staff of historians and journalists. Ford maintained that despite the organizational machinery his editorial procedures neither infringed upon the historians' freedom of interpretation nor inhibited their style. Had this been the situation, he argued, "none of those men would have touched the job with a 10-foot pole."[9]

Part of Ford's success in gaining a semblance of conformity

[7] Ford, "America's Fight for Public Opinion," *Minnesota History Bulletin* 3 (February 1919): 4-5.

[8] The NSL seemed to have fewer printing and scheduling problems than the CPI, which was using the already rushed facilities of the GPO.

[9] U. S., Congress, *Hearings, Sundry Civil Bill, 1919,* part 3, p. 107.

among his historians came from his method of delegation and his concern for historical accuracy. Most of the ideas for pamphlets originated in his office and went to a historian for execution. On occasion the NBHS would suggest a topic and offer its staff to implement it, and sometimes the CPI would reprint a pertinent article or speech appearing in another medium. These outside sources, however, contributed a small minority of the pamphlet ideas and underwent the same editorial treatment as the indigenous topics. By selecting an author for an approved idea, Ford could almost guarantee that results would conform to CPI principles. Fearing the damage that irresponsible propaganda could do to both the historians and the CPI, he instructed his assistants that "nothing is going to be printed or go out as a Government publication that is not so carefully done that you men will be willing to stand for it 20 years from now."[10]

Such long-term projections were foreign to McElroy's idea of propaganda. He maintained that "we do not know enough to speak as the historians of the future will speak, . . . we have not all of the facts, but we have enough to be certain that we are fighting for our national existence."[11] With this sense of urgency and with editorial procedures less rigid than Ford's, it is no wonder NSL pamphlets displayed greater diversity. McElroy acted more as a clearinghouse for ideas than as a technical editor and arbiter of standards. Several of the pamphlets appearing in the Patriotism Through Education Series were products of independent work which McElroy had agreed to publish with NSL sponsorship, even though their scholarly qualities frequently left much to be desired.

The pamphlets by CPI, NBHS, and NSL historians fell into three classifications. The first included those which affirmed the ideals of America and the Allies. The second showed unattractive aspects of the Central Powers and established German guilt for the war. The third classification included service-oriented literature, intended to make war activities personal by cataloging them and offering suggestions for civilian participation in the national

---

[10] Ibid., p. 99.
[11] *New York Times*, 9 September 1917, sec. 4, p. 5.

mobilization. These categories are arbitrary and not altogether inclusive, but will offer a convenient pattern for surveying the field. Very few of the pamphlets fit exclusively into one single group, and frequently the first and second categories overlapped by showing positive and negative features simultaneously.

The first category of pamphlets might appear to have been little more than an affirmation of innocence proven by American reluctance to enter a European war. It would appeal to the country's pride and mission to view this struggle as a crusade in which America came to the defense of democracy. White in a world mostly black, savior to a dying civilization, this image of America would require little documentation other than reference to patriotism, justice, and fair play. Historians in the three organizations were not content, however, to use this technique by itself. They supplemented this approach with collaborative material from international law, demographic traditions, and ideology. From American history they gleaned arguments to affirm the nation's innocence, neutrality, and faith in diplomatic arbitration and the hands-off policy of the Monroe Doctrine. They described the war in terms of democracy versus autocracy and pictured the Allies as traditional friends of America. Idealism permeated all these arguments; the pamphlets were openly Wilsonian in arming themselves with Christian righteousness and espousing a new international order for peace and understanding. Prose imagery remained one-sided and the general reasoning was simplistic and emotional, but the substantiating arguments displayed a wealth of selective research.

Considering the issues, it was only logical that the CPI's initial pamphlet would be an exegesis of Wilson's war address. As the world leader of democracy, Wilson had spoken eloquently in its behalf on April 2, and the *Literary Digest* called this speech "a mighty trumpet blast."[12] Ford was anxious to amplify the president's talk through the first CPI publication and called on his Minnesota colleague William Stearns Davis to annotate the address for popular circulation. Davis had already begun work along a similar line and welcomed Ford's invitation to transfer it into a

[12] *Literary Digest* 54 (21 April 1917): 1156.

government project.[13] He had been eager to offer his services in any capacity, fearing, like many nonmilitary men, that the war would pass him by. Author of several historical novels as well as European history surveys, he was known for his vivid, almost melodramatic, prose style, and this would seem to equip him well for dramatizing American intervention. Using materials and assistance available at the Minnesota campus, he had the pamphlet ready for distribution in early June to capitalize on the enthusiasm that marked America's entry in the war.

Entitled *The War Message and the Facts behind It*, the pamphlet reprinted Wilson's address with forty footnotes. Ford's introduction pointed out that the address "is the best possible preparation for all loyal Americans . . . who are trying to discover the proper mental attitude." To insure its proper interpretation Davis's footnotes expanded the twelve-page speech to twenty-eight pages and concentrated on dramatic proofs rather than subtleties. The majority of the notes were expository, referring readers to standard sources and pairing Wilson's rhetoric with Davis's research. Following the president's phrase, "American ships have been sunk, American lives taken," Davis listed ships and persons fallen victim of German attacks; after Wilson proclaimed that "the right is more precious than peace and we shall fight for the things which we have always carried nearest our hearts," Davis quoted from Lincoln's second inaugural address to delineate the American traditions involved, including charity and a lack of malice.[14] The technique evoked a dual response from readers: the president's words provided an emotional commitment to war, and Davis's footnotes offered the historical justification for belligerency.

McElroy's first pamphlet for the NSL did not bother with documentation but displayed another form of research—that of comparative quotations. *The Ideals of Our War* contained the outline for most of McElroy's speeches; even in pamphlet form its aggressive optimism had an oratorical air. Charging that "we are

---

[13] G. S. Ford, "Reminiscences," Columbia Oral History Collection, copy at University of Minnesota Library, 2: 373-74.

[14] CPI, War Information Series, no. 1 (Washington, D. C., 1917), pp. 9, 27-28.

not a modern Don Quixote wandering about the earth intent upon redressing imaginary wrongs. We are a peace-loving people," McElroy compared pacific quotations from Wilson with militarist quotations from German scholars and politicians. In six categories including equality of nations, free and open seas, and limitations on armaments, he paralleled Wilson's utterances with those of Nietzsche, Treitschke, and Frederick the Great. After allowing Wilson's pristine phrases to demolish their German counterparts in the verbal chess game, he concluded with an inevitable checkmate position. "The triumph of American ideals will mean . . . the deathknell of absolutism throughout the world."[15]

If this juxaposition of quotations offered comparative proof of American rightness, Andrew C. McLaughlin supplied another kind of evidence in his *The Great War: From Spectator to Participant*, that of the unanswered rhetorical question. An expert in constitutional history, McLaughlin developed his arguments in the casual yet confident manner of a lawyer convinced that his jury will pronounce the desired verdict if he gives them the proper evidence. After compiling an impressive list of German affronts to Allied honor he asked, "Was the world falling? Was civilization being wrecked in the whirlwind of barbaric passion?" He then concluded that America had entered the war because "Europe needed the assistance of an external power, disinterested and highhearted."[16] Shotwell responded to McLaughlin's didactic questions with the assessment that his technique was "bully through and through" and envisioned diverse uses for the pamphlet by other propagandists. Shortly after its publication it became a standard patriotic source that McLaughlin and others used repeatedly in speeches and articles to instruct public opinion.[17]

Whether historians chose to instruct readers with documentation, intrigue them with quotations, or quiz them rhetorically, all sought justification of American ideals. Still, an embarrassing facet of this affirmative pamphleteering was that the Allied and As-

---

[15] NSL, Patriotism Through Education Series, no. 5 (New York, 1917), pp. 7, 14.
[16] CPI, War Information Series, no. 4 (Washington D. C., 1917), pp. 9, 15.
[17] J. T. Shotwell to McLaughlin, June 1917, Box 3, Folder 2, McLaughlin Papers, University of Chicago Library. See also Box 7 for a collection of manuscripts illustrating the various uses made of this pamphlet.

sociated Powers had not shared common aims or enjoyed consistently friendly relations before 1917. British-American disputes in particular, such as the War of 1812, the Oregon Territory conflict, the *Alabama* claims, and the Alaskan border dispute, testified to a long history of dissension among the Anglo-Saxons. Rather than attempt a denial of this situation Claude H. Van Tyne admitted the problem and sought a solution. In his *Democracy's Education Problem* he asserted that part of the distrust between England and America came from failure to forget hatreds from the Revolutionary War. Prejudiced textbooks and professors had kept alive this distant source of conflict which among many Americans manifested itself as Anglophobic fears. Through a schoolroom routine that had overemphasized the brave colonial stand against the "redcoats" most students remained unaware of the innumerable cultural, economic, and political links between the two nations. "By nursing that ignorance and prejudice we have taught some seven or eight generations of Americans to hate England."[18] Van Tyne suggested changing textbooks and teachers' attitudes to emphasize for school children the common Anglo-American heritage and to correct the wrong views of those badly taught. Perhaps then, he hoped, after this war ended the two nations could resume their rightful places and sit together mother and daughter.

Within most of their publications the historians inserted idealism as if it were a required commodity. Almost every pamphlet advertised justice, brotherhood, decency, and democracy. Evarts B. Greene chronicled America's historic disinterest in the rivalries, the alliances, and the whole "system which has converted Europe into a group of armed camps." But when Europe's turmoil began to endanger the serenity of other continents, America could no longer remain disinterested, for "it is only in a *world* made safe for democracy that America herself can be safe and free."[19] Carl Becker's *America's War Aims and Peace Program* perhaps best shows the manner in which these historians adopted this attitude.

[18] NSL, Patriotism Through Education Series, no. 38 (New York, n.d. [probably early 1918]), p. 6.
[19] Greene, *America's Interest in Popular Government Abroad*, War Information Series, no. 8 (Washington, D. C., 1917), p. 16.

Even as editor of this brief anthology of writings, Becker revealed his alignment with Wilson's idealism. One editorial transition offered a key to his position:

> The entrance of the United States into the war, obviously without any desire for territorial or material advantages, but in defense of its own rights and for the vindication of just and humane principles, cleared the way for the renunciation, on the part of the Allies, of all imperialistic aims. More than ever before, the war came to be regarded as a clear cut conflict between two ideals—the ideal of democracy and the rights of people to determine their own way of life, over against the German ideal of a world empire established by ruthless aggression.[20]

With his usual methods, Ford circulated rough drafts of this pamphlet among several individuals for verification. One copy went to the president who returned it with the notation, "I have taken some liberties here and there with this, but send it back with my unhesitating approval."[21] Like the other affirmative pamphlets, this one emphasized optimistic ideals and anticipated a new international order.

For the historians, shifting from a defense of American aims to an accusation of German ideals proved easy. This task offered few difficulties because patterns of thought were already established. Since America had declared war on Germany, no one could doubt the enemy's identity, and because the Allies had subjected America to almost three years of propaganda, the material for this second category of pamphlets was available. A vocabulary of reproach had also embedded itself in American speech by the time of the nation's entry into war. "Hun," a generic reference to barbaric Germans; "boche," a derogatory appellation for German soldiers; "schrecklichkeit" (frightfulness) and "kultur" all called forth bestial ideals. The result was a policy that came to be known as "skinning of the kaiser."[22] McElroy displayed no compunction about condemning

---

[20] CPI, War Information Series, no. 21 (Washington, D. C., 1918), p. 12.

[21] Wilson to George Creel, 26 October 1918, Becker Papers, Collection of Regional History, John M. Olin Research Library, Cornell University.

[22] Charles D. Hazen to J. T. Shotwell, 3 July 1917, Box 3, NBHS Records.

German culture. The enemy should be attacked frontally because the German soul was "a soul perverted, and black as hell itself."[23] Ford preferred an indirect strategy. He decided that the most effective attack on such a foe would be to allow it to condemn itself by revealing its own methods, purposes, and guilt. Whether by indicting the Germans or by letting them incriminate themselves, the pamphlets achieved the same results. CPI and NSL historians concentrated on three ideas: that Germany was responsible for the war, had committed atrocities unbecoming a civilized nation, and offered a threat not only to the opposing European nations already on the field, but to American soil.

With unconscious irony the CPI chose material for its most popular accusatory pamphlet from the source that had provided material for its most popular affirmative pamphlet, a speech by Wilson. Ford delegated to another of his Minnesota colleagues the task of documenting the speech. This time the job went to Wallace Notestein, a young professor who was soon to establish his reputation as an authority on English history. Ford knew of his disappointment when he failed to get into the army because of a childhood crippling ailment. He also knew that Notestein had thoroughly researched the prewar pan-German movement and might be able to put this material to good use for the government. Ford wrote him that he had "been looking for something which would do as a text upon which we could hang a collection of excerpts from German publicists and newspapers. . . . The Flag Day speech [delivered June 14, 1917] has made that possible."[24] Notestein's annotation of *The President's Flag Day Address* appeared on September 15 and ultimately achieved a printing of 6,813,340 copies, far surpassing in circulation any other historian's war efforts.[25]

The address itself had arraigned the German government so severely that Wilson's adviser, Edward House, predicted Germany

[23] McElroy, *The Representative Idea and the War*, Patriotism Through Education Series, no. 24 (New York, 1917), p. 8; *New York Times*, 9 September 1917, sec. 4, p. 5.

[24] Ford to Notestein, 19 June 1917, 3-A1, Tray 1, CPI Records.

[25] CPI, Red, White, and Blue Series, no. 4 (Washington, D. C., 1917); CPI, *Complete Report*, pp. 15-16.

would need centuries to live down the indictment.[26] Notestein and his aides lengthened this indictment with twenty-four footnotes which paraphrased or quoted from German newspapers, speeches, correspondence, and periodicals. When Wilson accused Germany of inciting Mexico against America, Notestein reprinted portions of the Zimmermann telegram; when Wilson stated that Germany had long desired and planned for war, Notestein offered quotations from thirteen German politicians and writers. This excerpt from *Jung Deutschland*—the official publication of the Young German League—was typical: "War is the noblest and holiest expression of human activity. For us, too, the glad, great hour of battle will strike." At times the annotation moved independently of the text. One footnote deprecated Germany's peace overtures and predicted that Germany would "continue to offer baits for peace—a peace that means 'rectification of frontiers' in her favor."[27] By the end of the pamphlet it was clear that Wilson's address had served only as cue lines in this litany of German self-incrimination.

The success of this technique apparently convinced Ford that German testimonials were strong enough to stand without assistance. *Conquest and Kultur: Aims of the Germans in Their Own Words* resulted in 160 pages of German quotations, edited, arranged, and indexed. Such was Ford's delight that his usual reserve deserted him when he wrote in the introduction, "The pied pipers of Prussianism who have led the German people to conquest and to ignominy and to infamy are here given their unending day before the court of public opinion. It is a motley throng who are here heard in praise of war and international suspicion and conquest and intrigue and devastation."[28] Arranged under headings such as "The Worship of Power" and "Pretexts for War," the quotations ranged from two lines to several pages, and the majority contained a plethora of ellipses, leaving only the truncated portions to present their abbreviated messages. Pertinent phrases,

26 Charles Seymour, ed., *The Intimate Papers of Colonel House*, 4 vols. (Boston, 1926-1928), 3: 137.

27 Notestein, *The President's Flag Day Address*, pp. 15, 26.

28 CPI, Red, White, and Blue Series, no. 5 (Washington, D. C., 1917). Notestein received editorial assistance from nine other historians in compiling this anthology.

set in bold type to enhance their visual impact, emphasized salient points of duplicity or bestiality. The serried ranks of quotations presented a swaggering display of incrimination and the editors provided additional testimony with vignettes of the most frequently quoted sources. Kaiser Wilhelm II appeared at least twelve times with such utterances as "I shall stand no nonsense from America after the war." Heinrich von Treitschke, the historian of Bismarck's day, appeared nine times with "blood and iron" adages; Frederick the Great espoused militarism six times; Nietzsche expounded his philosophical worship of war; and Friedrich von Bernhardi, the soldier-scholar, advocated Germany's "place in the sun" sixteen times.

The simplistic impression made by these selected testimonials fulfilled the requirements of propaganda but went further toward branding the German people than Notestein, and perhaps even Ford, had intended. Whenever possible Ford tried to maintain the Wilsonian dichotomy that America was waging war against the German state rather than the German people. But the pressures of time and brevity in pamphlet production often blurred distinctions between the two. Notestein included in the original draft of *Conquest and Kultur* several references to German antiwar groups and civilians who opposed the policies of their kaiser and military leaders. cpi editors deleted these references before the final proofs, partly bcause they blunted the impact of the collection and partly because they might draw attention to Notestein's name, which was German. As for Notestein, he objected to the ommission and even suggested having his name removed from the pamphlet, but to no avail. Both Ford and Jameson argued that a pamphlet with an anonymous author would lack credibility. Notestein agonized over this episode for some time and sent a copy of the pamphlet to his Yale professor, George Burton Adams, describing the situation and explaining that he did not want to embarrass his mentor with his cpi involvement. "I have often wondered what you would think of this kind of work—propaganda work—whether a scholar should do it or not. . . . I hope the text and notes are accurate and fair. I have tried hard to make them so." Adams reassured him that the pamphlet was well done and that the appearance of his

name on it would not affect his reputation as a scholar.[29] Fifty
years later Notestein still regretted the pamphlet's oversimplified
attack on Germans, but admitted that the CPI probably meant
well.[30]

Ford found it difficult to resolve this dilemma of either being
too lenient on the Germans or overemphasizing negative aspects
of their culture, and the results of trying to strike a compromise
often pleased no one. Early in the war Ford thought that a pamphlet describing the German military code, quoting from the official military manuals, would be an effective means to reveal German aggressiveness. But as this pamphlet took shape under the
guidance of James W. Garner of the University of Illinois, Ford
began to doubt its effectiveness. "War codes," he decided, "even
in humane nations, are likely to contain things which taken out
of their texts and apart from the spirit in which they are executed,
sound quite as barbaric as similar passages in the Prussian War
Code."[31] Despite his reservations, *The German War Code* finally
materialized to unmask German "brutality, ruthlessness, terrorism,
and violence" and Ford apparently had to accept the compromises
which pamphleteering made necessary.[32]

Thomas Moran of Purdue University intensified the attack on
German ideals by combining German testimonials with hypothetical situations in his NSL pamphlet *Ten Fundamental War Principles*. Although his ten principles were indistinct, the message was
clear: Germans were a brutal people. Quoting from one of the
kaiser's speeches to his soldiers, he let Wilhelm incriminate himself with one of the most frequently reprinted quotations of the
war: "When you meet the foe you will defeat him. No quarter
will be given; no prisoners will be taken. Let all who fall into your
hands be at your mercy. Just as the Huns a thousand years ago,
under the leadership of Attila, gained a reputation in virtue of
which they still live in historical tradition, so may the name of
Germany become known." Moran saw the threat to American

---

[29] Notestein to Adams, 27 November 1917, and Adams to Notestein, 4 December
1917, Folder 265, George Burton Adams Papers, Yale University Library.

[30] Notestein to author, 27 August 1967.

[31] Ford to Garner, 7 June 1917, 3-Al, Tray 1, CPI Records.

[32] CPI, War Information Series, no. 11 (Washington, D. C., 1918), p. 2.

security in terms designed to start farmers practicing maneuvers on courthouse lawns. He pictured the enemy "coming across the Rio Grande and sweeping up through the Middle West. Which would you rather do—fight the Germans in Indiana and Illinois or fight them on the western front . . .?"[33]

Earl E. Sperry of Syracuse University chose to fight them on the homefront but he regarded the most imminent threat as civilians rather than soldiers. In his heavily documented *The Tentacles of the German Octopus in America* he classified German-American newspapers, clubs, schools, and churches as dangerous appendages of the German government. Because of their cultural and linguistic ties to the homeland, these organizations constituted a divisive force and prevented assimilation of immigrants. Whether pro-German or not, they were "a detriment to America. Our national life will be stronger, sounder, and healthier without them."[34] Sperry found a receptive audience for this punitive Americanization and all three groups of historians continued his domestic "search and destroy" mission. The CPI published a similar exposé by Sperry, *German Plots and Intrigues*,[35] showing examples of German subversion in America, and Shotwell encouraged some of his students to assist the NSL and CPI in collecting material for these and similar pamphlets.[36]

Evarts B. Greene, the new chairman of the NBHS in late 1917, regretted these attacks on German culture and the resultant guilt-by-association that loyal German-Americans acquired. He convinced Ford that a pamphlet should emphasize German contributions to American culture to offset the persecutions of American citizens with German backgrounds. Hence, Greene's *Lieber and Schurz: Two Loyal Americans of German Birth* traced the political and reform activities of two immigrants to show that the threat to America came not from peoples but from governments. Describing their work in the abolition movement, Francis Lieber's writing

[33] NSL, Patriotism Through Education Series, no. 32 (New York, n.d.), pp. 4, 7. At least four CPI pamphlets reprinted the kaiser's statement in full; others used it in part or reference.

[34] NSL, Patriotism Through Education Series, no. 21 (New York, n.d.), p. 19.

[35] CPI, Red, White, and Blue Series, no. 10 (Washington, D. C., 1918).

[36] Harry Elmer Barnes to author, 13 April 1968.

assignments for President Lincoln, and Carl Schurz's service in the Union army, Greene attempted to place them in the American mainstream and allay the "indiscriminate distrust and ill-will toward the German-born population."[37] It was only a cautious polishing of the melting pot's tarnished appearance, for the cpi published fewer copies of this pamphlet than of any other by its historians. Greene's motives were noble in their desire to soften national stereotypes; his results, however, were minimal. In a time when most Americans saw issues in black and white, he asked for a consideration of gray, something that required more tolerance than was available.

No matter how the pamphlets established German guilt, brutality, and subversion, they did not satisfy demands for horror and sensation. From Lincoln, Nebraska, a postmaster wrote that he wanted to see in print "that the Germans have bombed hospitals, killed Red Cross workers, raped Belgian women and girls."[38] A newspaper editor from Adrian, Michigan, demanded "the revival of the news value of the older atrocities."[39] In short, a market existed for an American version of the English Bryce Report. Scholars later discredited Lord Bryce's 300-page compendium of German atrocities for its sensationalism and unverified material, but it received credence when it appeared in 1915. The former ambassador's name lent respectability to this grisly account of tortures, mutilations, rapes, and other violations of decency that were, for the most part, documented only casually. Americans were psychologically disposed to accept its verdict and even the usually skeptical *Nation* ceased doubting the stories of German terrorism.[40] cpi and nsl pamphleteers referred to the report many times and described other similar incidents, but not until America's second year in the war did any American pamphlets give sustained coverage to atrocities.

Somewhat reluctantly, Ford asked Dana C. Munro, the distinguished medievalist, to undertake the chore of authenticating atrocity reports for the American public. He instructed him to

---

[37] cpi, War Information Series, no. 19 (Washington, D. C., 1918), p. 3.
[38] W. Cipra to George Creel, 29 August 1918, 3-A1, Tray 19, cpi Records.
[39] S. H. Perry to cpi, 4 December 1917, 3-A1, Tray 8, cpi Records.
[40] *Nation* 100 (20 May 1915): 554-55.

unmask or substantiate the accounts that came from the Bryce Report and other sources but not to include any material that would not "stand up in court."[41] Wartime restrictions limited Munro and his two assistants, George C. Sellery from Wisconsin and August C. Krey from Minnesota, to material in American archives and published reports from available witnesses. They hesitated to print testimony they could not verify, and when they did include secondary accounts they accompanied them with editorial explanations which generally had the effect of lessening their shock appeal or questioning their reliability. The results of this work, *German War Practices*,[42] in the opinion of another CPI pamphleteer, "gave little support to the long-believed catalogue of disorderly and brutal private crimes."[43]

The pamphlet promised more than it delivered. Passages from the Bryce Report, the German *White Book* of diplomatic documents, and Ambassador James Gerard's *My Four Years in Germany* were familiar stories. Descriptions by relief workers in Belgium, such as Herbert Hoover, Brand Whitlock, and Vernon Kellogg, were poignant but they told only of the effects of alleged atrocities. The pamphlet gave the impression of being secondhand accounts written in the passive voice by editors not convinced. Probably aware that readers would be disappointed, the editors enlivened their work with variations in typography and layout. Headlines such as WANTON DESTRUCTION or DEPORTATIONS AND FORCED LABOR promised interesting reading, yet introduced ordinary reports of ruined cathedrals and displaced persons. Marginal comments of "Graves of the Dead" suggested more than was revealed in their accompanying paragraphs, which described village cemeteries. Ironically, this CPI project could have been strident in its sensationalism and proved to be among the tamest of the historians' pamphlets.

Neither positive nor negative in tone, the third classification of pamphlets sought to inform and assist the public. These presented

41 Ford, "Reminiscences," 2: 383.
42 CPI, Red White, and Blue Series, nos. 6 and 8 (Washington, D. C., 1918). The project appeared in two pamphlets, bearing the subtitles *Treatment of Civilians* and *German Treatment of Conquered Territory*.
43 Frederick L. Paxson, *American Democracy and the World War*, 3 vols. (Boston, 1936-1948), 1: 169.

catalogs of international statistics, descriptions of wartime bureaus and agencies, and opportunities for readers to "do their bit" in the war effort. Probably because the CPI had access to government information, its pamphlets were more comprehensive than most of those from the NSL, but both groups of historians acted as clearinghouses for service-oriented material.

Two pamphlets by the CPI and the NSL offered brief lessons in politics and ethnology. Charles D. Hazen of Harvard delivered in his *The Government of Germany*[44] a sixteen-page analysis of the German political and constitutional structure that could well have been a lecture in comparative government. In didactic prose he outlined the powers of the German government, analyzed voter distribution in the German states, described the traditional dominance of Prussia in the bicameral legislature, and offered an occasional reprimand to the monarchs for treating their constitution as a "scrap of paper." On the whole, the pamphlet was circumspect, aimed more at instructing than converting its readers. Likewise, Earl Sperry's *Tentacles of the German Octopus* offered a handy compilation of German-American organizations and activities. Although condemnatory in tone, its lists and descriptions made it a much-used reference source on German religion, journalism, and social life.

While other historians were producing small topical pamphlets for public service, A. B. Hart undertook a massive catalog of wartime information that consumed his prodigious energies as well as those of the NSL staff. Entitled *America at War: A Handbook of Patriotic Educational References*,[45] it was a 400-page omnium gatherum, too bulky to be a handbook and too immediate to be anything other than a pamphlet. Hart included information and suggestions applicable to almost every age, educational level, and emotional commitment to the war. For the passive reader there were lists of war novels, brief histories of the belligerent nations, and bibliographies on innumerable subjects; for the active participant the handbook supplied the names and activities of private, local, state, and federal agencies that welcomed volunteer help,

[44] CPI, War Information Series, no. 3 (Washington, D. C., 1917).
[45] NSL, Committee on Patriotism Through Education (New York, 1918).

and encouraged patriots to use the assembled outlines and quotations for speeches and debates. It was the League's most ambitious pamphlet and probably its most valuable service during the war. No other publication of wartime material was as direct or helpful with its guidelines for civilian participation. Unfortunately, because of its size and late appearance in 1918, it received less use than it deserved.

The CPI's *War Cyclopedia: A Handbook for Ready Reference on the Great War*[46] offered a compilation of aids similar to Hart's *Handbook*. Put together by more than twenty historians this 321-page pamphlet contained maps, chronological charts, bibliographies, and a maze of cross-references to its hundreds of vignettes, definitions, and work guidelines. To edit this arsenal of facts and suggestions Ford chose Frederick L. Paxson of the University of Wisconsin and secured for his assistance Samuel B. Harding, Edwin S. Corwin, and Bernadotte E. Schmitt. Paxson asked other historians to prepare brief essays from an assigned list of terms and his staff then edited and arranged these in the style of a "party campaign text-book."[47] From Charles A. Beard he solicited discussion of "atrocities," "Rheims," and "frightfulness," and Sidney B. Fay contributed descriptive essays on "Berlin to Bagdad," "Place in the Sun," and "Bernhardi." Becker, Jameson, Dodd, Munro, Notestein, Carl Russell Fish, and many others provided additional material. The assembled items displayed at the same time pro-American and anti-German overtones, but the bulk of the material was practical, nonideological information such as this discussion of "Food Economy Campaigns": "A 'wheatless' day each week will go far to effect the saving of food necessary to win the war. . . . The man who buys because he has money and wastes because he can afford to is helping the enemy. . . . Enlist in the food campaign and then obey orders like a good soldier."[48]

The *War Cyclopedia* proved so helpful in imposing a form of order on the myriad war activities that the CPI decided to revise it for a second edition. The November 1918 armistice forestalled

[46] CPI, Red, White, and Blue Series, no. 7 (Washington, D. C., 1918).

[47] Frederick L. Paxson, CPI circular letters, August 1917, 3-A1, Tray 24, CPI Records.

[48] CPI, *War Cyclopedia*, p. 97.

the project, however, and Samuel Harding's revised version remained unpublished. The pamphlet also proved helpful in rescuing the reputations of several historians who were under attack for seeming to be unenthusiastic about the Allied cause. Ford distributed to these men small assignments for the *Cyclopedia* and then announced that they were doing patriotic work for the federal government. For historians such as Charles A. Beard—whose championship of free speech made him suspect—these small public favors relieved much of the intimidation that anti-German organizations were applying.[49]

NSL and CPI-NBHS pamphlets shared many themes and editorial techniques. They reduced war issues to black and white, infused idealism and righteousness into America's role, and established German guilt with finality. Whether in exhortations, documented essays, or guidelines for civilian activism these pamphlets succeeded as propaganda. The frequency with which magazines and newspapers reprinted them and the difficulty which their sponsors had in meeting circulation demands testify to their acceptability. It is doubtful that these historians of 1917-1918 considered their pamphlets serious contributions to knowledge. The purpose of their existence and the manner of presentation identified them as nonscholarly works for the public. Juxtaposition of selective quotations, at which McElroy excelled, and Moran's use of hypothetical situations presented dramatic cases but were dubious practices from the viewpoint of historical objectivity. Even the more intricate use of documentation and bibliographies seen in Davis's, Sperry's, and Notestein's pamphlets did not substitute for genuine research; indeed, many footnotes in the CPI pamphlets referred readers to other CPI pamphlets.

Despite similarities between their pamphlets and occasional cooperative circulation campaigns, friction developed between some of the NSL historians and their colleagues in the CPI and NBHS. Arising partly from personal reasons and partly from misgivings about professional ethics the friction received only a brief public exposure but revealed a division among the historians which

---

[49] Ford, "Reminiscences," 2: 395.

paralleled the varied constituencies of the three groups. This situation began at the NSL Speaker's Training Camp in July 1917, as John Latane waved in the air a copy of the CPI's *The War Message* and charged that it was "so full of errors in fact and inference that it is an insult to the intelligence of the American people. It is garbled as badly as the German publications which we have condemned." Hart supplemented Latane's charge with a terse "It is a poor job," and said that the pamphlet contained many misrepresentations. A lively discussion followed in which NSL delegates adopted a resolution criticizing the government for attempting this sort of propaganda.[50]

The incident caught the CPI unprepared. Since early June, "peach baskets" of mail had applauded *The War Message* and now other historians began attacking it. An apology from the League president admitted that he did not know "whether the critics are right or wrong"; he did, however, lament the outburst and the publicity.[51] Latane and William Stearns Davis, who was chiefly responsible for the pamphlet, carried on a lengthy correspondence, charging increasingly serious crimes of commission and omission. Both excelled at sarcasm and throughout the summer labeled each other as dangerously careless and scholarly incompetent, and indicted their respective committees for exposing nonexistent Gunpowder Plots and staging cheap and unnecessary public executions.[52] Ford assumed a hostile attitude toward the assailants. He dismissed Latane as a small and vindictive person who was part of a "group that sought controversy for controversy's sake," and protested that the pamphlet had not been for scholarly dissection; it was directed at a public not expecting all the apparatus of a learned monograph.[53] Shotwell felt no need to defend the scholastic standards of a propaganda tract, but did react with some petulance to the etiquette of his colleagues in the NSL: "I think that it would be a much more patriotic thing for Hart to do to cooperate with us . . . than for him to criticise in public and in a hostile spirit. . . .

[50] *New York Times,* 4 July 1917, p. 2.
[51] S. Stanwood Menken to G. S. Ford, 5 July 1917, 3-A1, Tray 20, CPI Records.
[52] Latane to Davis, 14 July, 21 July, 18 August 1917, Correspondence Folder, 1914-1917, Davis Papers.
[53] Ford to George Creel, 25 July 1917, 3-A1, Tray 1, CPI Records.

I think Hart's criticisms should have come to us before they were given to the syndicated press of the country. That is to me a failure in cooperation which extends beyond the range of mere scientific criticism."[54] Hart regretted the rancor that had developed among his friends and he apologized to Davis for the personal affronts associated with the episode. As for Latane, Hart said he would have to "fight his own battles."[55]

Latane continued to fight alone and carried the controversy to the *American Historical Review* where the criticism became more specific. In a seven-page letter intended for publication, he accused the work of the CPI-NBHS historians of being "thoroughly discreditable to American scholarship," and listed several "palpable errors and inaccuracies." Showing how the pamphlet footnotes had misquoted Washington's inaugural addresses, he concluded: "I was under the impression that the methods of Jared Sparks had long ago been repudiated and abandoned by historical scholars." He presented another example of editorial laxity with a word-by-word scrutiny of one footnote: "Now Lincoln did not say 'let us finish the work,' but 'let us strive on to finish the work.' He did not say 'to bind up another's wounds,' but 'to bind up the nation's wounds.' He did not say 'his widow and orphans,' but 'his widow and his orphan,' " Much of Latane's anger centered on the use of the 1900 United States Naval Code which the pamphlet had quoted to show how much more humane American maritime practices were than those of Germany. According to Latane the quotation was not only badly garbled but the code had been revoked in 1904 and should never have been quoted, even if correctly.[56]

Obviously chagrined at these criticisms leveled at his friends, Jameson returned Latane's letter and informed him that there was little point in the *Review* giving his opinions any more publicity than they had already received in the newspapers.[57] But later that week in a more conciliatory mood he asked a friend, "Why did nobody have the intelligence to put him [Latane] on the

[54] J. T. Shotwell to Arthur I. Andrews, 27 July 1917, Box 1, NBHS Records.
[55] Hart to Davis, n.d., Correspondence Folder, 1914-1917, Davis Papers.
[56] Latane to editor, AHR, 15 August 1917 (copy), Box 4, NBHS Records.
[57] Jameson to Latane, 25 August 1917 (copy), Box 4, NBHS Records.

Board!"[58] Ten months after the initial controversy Ford continued to distrust Latane and his "strict constructionist" associates in the NSL. "To put it colloquially, Latane is a chronic sore-head with practically no following of any sort in the historical profession."[59]

Latane's participation in this episode reopened a personal rift among historians that had existed for some years. He had been one of the ringleaders in a 1913 revolt against election procedures in the American Historical Association and conservative, "repressive" leadership in the profession. During the annual meeting held in Charleston, South Carolina, that year, he had succeeded in bringing the revolt to an open debate. The divisiveness continued for several months as the various factions debated in the pages of *The Nation*, involving personalities as well as issues. Although the revolt subsided with little consequence, many historians believed that the disturbance had been unjustified and malicious. Jameson felt that the insurgents had unfairly attacked his integrity, and Evarts B. Greene—normally a gentle person—threatened to ostracize Latane if he appeared at the next meeting of the association.[60] Ford and Shotwell fell in line with their friends and when historians began to join organizations for war work in 1917 it would seem that Latane's arrival at the NSL rather than the CPI or NBHS was no idle coincidence. He had conspicuously exempted Hart from his criticisms during the 1914 exchanges and the leadership of the CPI and NBHS represented many of his old antagonists.[61] The *War Message* imbroglio brought the former battle lines forward again.

Beyond baring personal animosities this friction also brought to light several other problems affecting historian pamphleteers. Editorial standards came under closer supervision to prevent a recurrence of such textual and interpretive errors. The *War Message* pamphlet reappeared in a revised edition and Hart quickly

[58] Jameson to McLaughlin, 30 August 1917 (copy), Box 63, File 1081, Jameson Papers, Manuscript Division, Library of Congress.

[59] Ford to Harvey O'Higgins, 31 May 1918, 3-A2, Tray 2, CPI Records.

[60] Waldo G. Leland, "Reminiscences," pp. 27-28, Columbia Oral History Collection, Columbia University.

[61] *Nation* 98 (26 February 1914): 207.

relayed his approval to Ford, thus easing some of the intergroup tensions.[62] The omnipresent question, however, received no answer: Were scholarship and patriotic service reconcilable? In this instance, several tentative answers arose as crisis palliatives, none of them satisfactory nor completely convincing to the profession. Having no precedents for wartime pamphleteering, these professors had surveyed arbitrary boundaries around history and propaganda; lacking a consensus on where to locate the lines, they created boundaries that overlapped and their pamphlets had to survive the crossfire from competitive organizations. What could have been a cooperative phalanx of pamphlets became an uncoordinated series of historical potshots.

[62] Ford to wife, 10 September 1917, Folder 165, Ford Papers, University of Minnesota Library.

IV. Using & Abusing Oratory

With a flourish of adjectives in his pamphlet entitled *Speakers Training Camp*, Professor A. B. Hart predicted a wartime speaker's crusade "as deep as the danger, as wide as the country, as high as the patriotic spirit of the people." As an oracle he proved accurate. Possibilities for oratory were great in an age when radio broadcasts were dimly feasible and "talkies" had not yet come to the cinema palaces. Mechanical amplification and recordings had not desiccated the art of public speaking and politicians as well as other public figures needed to make a good speech, delivered with grace and skill. To facilitate this need, most schools offered classes in elocution and declamation, training students in the basics of verbal as well as written rhetorical techniques. The popular Chautauqua circuits served as an apex to this training. Long a bastion of entertainment and learning, they offered a forum of oratorical excellence, lionizing and stimulating public lecturers. As in the nineteenth century, America in the early twentieth was a nation conditioned by oratory and would present a ready audience for wartime speakers.

The CPI's Four Minute Men were a logical product of this tradition and became the most specacular orators of the war. Sometimes called the "Stentorian Guard," these 75,000 volunteers ranged as far as Hart predicted, giving more than 7,500,000 speeches to a total audience estimated at 130,000,000.[1] Hardly a theater, church, or civic gathering escaped their exhortations to buy Liberty Bonds, conserve food and fuel, and support other campaigns. They made their presence so strongly felt that one journalist later wrote, "It became difficult for half a dozen persons to come together without having a Four Minute Man descend upon them . . . their aggregate voices turned on as if by spigot."[2] The seeming spontaneity of this young army belied the organizing efforts that contributed heavily to its success. The CPI published the *Four Minute Men Bulletin*, a kind of news sheet that coordinated topics,

speakers, and schedules. This brief periodical organized the requests and suggestions of many government agencies and disseminated them simultaneously to all parts of the nation through
the volunteer speakers. Ford and his staff of historians were instrumental in publishing the *Bulletin,* and with their editorial work
participated vicariously in wartime oratory.

Historians also participated directly in the verbal deluge of the
era and if their efforts were not as spectacular as those of the Four
Minute Men, they were more sustained. They raised considerably
the decibel count of war mobilization and stepped forward from
the relative anonymity of their pamphlets into the not-always-
pleasant glare of public life. The historians' speeches resembled
their pamphlets in that they displayed only a slight scholarship
and much use of Germanophobia. Their speeches differed from
their pamphlets, however, because the individual quality of oratory
revealed more personal temperaments and aimed at creating immediate excitement rather than systematic instruction. Robert
M. McElroy probably understood the ephemeral nature of oratory
as well as any of the historians. He acknowledged the limited
effect of a propaganda speech and coached his associates in ways
of obtaining repercussions that extended beyond the limits of their
audiences. Perhaps as a result, nsl speakers became more conspicuous than other scholarly orators, staying in the public eye
and commanding advance newspaper publicity and coverage. They
often found themselves the subjects of public debate and controversy.[3]

McElroy's instructions came from experience. He had early
established a habit of providing exciting copy for newspaper
columns; his use of shock, surprise, and humor made life easy
for headline composers and enhanced his reputation as a speaker.
He once told a crowd at a Baltimore country club that he wanted
to see the Allies march into Berlin and throw a lariat around the

[1] George Creel, *How We Advertised America* (New York, 1920), p. 85.

[2] Mark Sullivan, *Over Here, 1914-1918,* vol. 5 in *Our Times: The United States,
1900-1925,* 6 vols. (New York, 1926-1935), p. 432.

[3] McElroy's speeches and written work possessed a continuity rare among the
historians. Many of his pamphlets and articles were based on his stock speeches,
indicating that he wrote with an oratorical flavor.

statue of Frederick the Great.[4] This item from his repertoire became a favorite and audiences and reporters came to anticipate its use. In a New York address he kept the imagery but changed the geography by aiming at a similar statue of the Prussian monarch in Washington, D. C. "I mean to keep at the matter until the statue of Frederick the Vile is melted into bullets for use on the firing line over there."[5] Switching from light topical humor to German gore was another McElroy technique for unsettling audiences. One example which he used in endless variations was to recite "real poems of the German soul" such as

> I have slaughtered the old and the sorrowful;
> I have struck off the breasts of women;
> And I have run through the bodies of children
> Who gazed up at me with the eyes of a wounded lion.[6]

These items were predictable in most McElroy performances and their effect on audiences almost measurable, leading some reporters to compare results of the same presentations on different audiences, thus giving McElroy added publicity.

William Roscoe Thayer and Samuel B. Harding employed less humor than McElroy but they had been shocking audiences since the European war began and winning the requisite newspaper space. Thayer introduced his speeches by insulting audiences and then tossing anti-German statements into their agitated midst, hoping that an aroused audience would be more receptive than a passive one. Following a speech in 1916 he wrote, "It was a strangely exhilarating sensation, to stand up there in the presence of 3,000 persons, not knowing whether they would mob you or not. . . . It was probably not politic or philosophical; but . . . my middle name is not 'discretion.' "[7] Harding's version of the same technique made him a popular speaker in the Midwest and he became an indefatigable traveler and lecturer. Describing a tour

[4] *Baltimore American*, 6 October 1917.
[5] *New York Tribune*, 8 February 1918, and *Philadelphia Public Ledger*, 10 February 1918.
[6] *New York Times*, 6 September 1917, p. 1.
[7] Thayer to Mrs. Michael Foster, 6 March 1916, in Charles D. Hazen, ed., *The Letters of William Roscoe Thayer* (Boston, 1926), p. 276.

through Southern Indiana in a Ford, a hack, a trolley, and the B & O and Big Four railroads, he decided that "it was worth all the trouble to get a chance to shake my fist in the faces of the Germans . . . and damn the Kaiser."[8]

Hart and Ford proved equally adept at arousing emotions and expanding the effects of their speeches beyond the immediate listeners. Taking occasional leaves from their official duties, they managed to supplement their brief appearances with tangential controversies that indirectly increased the size of their audiences. In what appeared to be a master-stroke of stage management, Hart transformed a serene forum at New York City's Church of the Ascension into a shouting brawl, the echoes of which reverberated in the newspapers for days. After lecturing on American ideals in the war he accepted questions from the floor, one of which turned out to be an anti-Wilson harangue. Hart immediately jumped to his feet, leveled his finger at the questioner, and shouted, "I won't give anybody in the world a chance to say that I sat still and took that! . . . It is outright sedition."[9] The ensuing discussion on freedom of speech departed from the scheduled topic of the forum, but gained immeasurable publicity for Hart.

Ford accomplished a similar feat in Salt Lake City the following spring. While addressing a capacity audience at the Mormon Tabernacle, he deviated from his usual presentation on politics and diplomacy to attack the morality of the German government. He reviewed examples of dishonesty, deceit, and destruction of churches and convents, and concluded that Germany was an irreligious state "without a soul," committing sacrilege under the guise of righteousness.[10] This injection of religion into wartime oratory raised so many questions about its propriety that Ford later admitted he was henceforth "all for letting the Kaiser monopolize God in this war, at least so far as governmental propaganda is concerned."[11]

[8] Harding to Ford, 18 October 1917, 3-A1, Tray 4, cpi Records.
[9] *New York Times*, 25 June 1917, p. 11.
[10] *Salt Lake Tribune*, 18 May 1918, clipping in Folder 28, Ford Papers, University of Minnesota Library.
[11] Ford to George Creel, 24 July 1918 (copy), 3-A2, Tray 1, cpi Records.

Individual historians continued their personal lecturing throughout the war but the collective enterprises of the NSL, CPI, and NBHS reached broader audiences in their efforts to assist and educate rather than merely arouse. Through organized group activity they presented historical lecture series that followed consistent themes in all sections of the nation simultaneously. They also offered their service in a more silent fashion to other volunteer orators by means of speakers' handbooks and visual aids. And by sponsoring an international exchange of historians to lecture on Allied aims and ideals, they carried their propaganda messages even closer to the center of the military holocaust. This systematic approach to oratory further revealed the differences of personality within the three groups, the NSL producing more instant attention and the CPI and NBHS engineering a quieter and more prolonged approach.

Working on the assumption that legions of volunteers would give out much unsound information, the NSL attempted to forestall errors by supplying a compendium of "sound" information in their *Handbook of the War for Public Speakers.* At twenty-five cents, this repository became so popular that the NSL issued a revised, expanded version in the second year of the war.[12] Hart explained that these booklets were published "in the belief that there is an opportunity throughout the country to impress people by word of mouth." Newspapers and other publications were serving heroic purposes in spreading information, yet public meetings and personal contacts contributed a special kind of publicity unmatched in printed sources. To expedite this process the handbooks were to be "carried in the pocket, read on the cars, and used as a source of arguments and a reservoir of quotations."[13]

These two speakers' aids provided scores of militant speech outlines supplemented with songs, poems, quotations, and bibliographies. Cross-references and indexes offered rapid assistance for the unprepared speaker in constructing different kinds of speeches for various occasions. Speech outlines, such as "German Fright-

---

[12] Hart, ed. (New York, 1917); idem, *America at War* (New York, 1918). Arthur Lovejoy of Johns Hopkins assisted Hart with these handbooks.
[13] Hart, *America at War*, pp. iv-v.

fulness in General" and "Time for National Grit," indicated the anti-German and practical nature of the topics, and quotations from German and American dignitaries offered evidence of irresponsibility and honor which the speaker could insert at appropriate spots. After the war Hart told a Senate subcommittee that he felt no compunction about the oversimplifications and biases in the handbooks because he believed that oral propaganda required argument uncluttered with academic alternatives. If the books could have made "a greater appeal for protecting the United States and civilization against the Germans then I was at fault, because that is what I meant to put in those books."[14] One postwar critic of this Germanophobia estimated that Hart's speech handbooks "had a bigger circulation during 1917-1918 than any other patriotic work."[15] If this estimate is accurate the printing would have exceeded the 6,000,000 copies of the CPI's most popular item, no mean achievement.

Not content to act as an ammunition dump for orators, the NSL organized its own forensic army for a more consistent and tightly controlled attack on public opinion. During Hart's chairmanship his committee distributed a printed brochure entitled "Outline of Plan for Public Addresses and Lectures" which described the League's available services. It urged churches, schools, civic groups, and other organizations to sponsor NSL speakers for talks on any of forty-odd topics. The speakers were available as individuals or teams and came equipped with posters, slides, maps, and charts according to the nature of the speech.[16] During the first months of the war the NSL mailed from thirty to fifty letters a day to advertise its services and recruit new speakers for its roster, which already exceeded 500 scholars from more than 100 colleges and universities.[17]

Among these 500 speakers was an "elite corps" of historians

[14] U. S., Congress, Senate, *Brewing and Liquor Interests and German Propaganda: Hearings before a Subcommittee on the Judiciary*, 65 Cong., 2 and 3 sess. (Washington, D. C., 1919), 2: 1626.

[15] Charles Angoff, "The Higher Learning Goes to War," *American Mercury* 11 (June 1927): 181-82.

[16] NSL, "Speaker Brochure" (New York, 1917), n.p.

[17] Henry L. West, *The Work of the National Security League* (New York, 1917), n.p.

which conducted a propaganda lecture series more intensive in scope than that of the regular League orators. The NSL had circulated a resolution requesting colleges and universities to donate members of their faculties for patriotic propaganda work.[18] Few schools could comply with this request, but from the largesse of those that could came professors Ephraim D. Adams of Stanford, Claude H. Van Tyne of Michigan, William B. Munro of Harvard, and Franklin H. Giddings of Columbia. McElroy divided the country into regions and assigned each historian to one of them for extensive engagements. As often as possible he transferred historians from their home sections into another, hoping that the unfamiliarity of new audiences would challenge the historians into sharper performances and that larger audiences would assemble for speakers from distant locations. Munro and Adams were good examples of the success of this plan. Working the Far West, Munro toured and lectured throughout California bearing his Harvard credentials as a symbol of the two coasts unified during the war. Likewise, Adams brought his California experiences to New England and did such energetic work that Tufts University awarded him an honorary degree in the spring of 1918.[19]

Van Tyne's part in this elite corps revealed much about NSL organization and procedures. McElroy departed from the usual plan and assigned Van Tyne to his home region, the old Northwest Territory, and informed the area's editors, educators, and civic leaders of his availability. From forthcoming invitations Van Tyne chose locations where he wished to speak and arranged his schedule with the host groups. In keeping with the patriotic volunteerism of the war years, these historians received no pay for their lecturing although the sponsoring audiences were expected to cover expenses. In many cases when local groups found themselves financially embarrassed after hosting a speaker, the League would supply the balance. Occasionally Van Tyne's transportation from one speaking engagement to another was made possible only by wiring McElroy's office in New York for emergency funds after a scheduled

18 *New York Times,* 4 November 1917, sec. 1, p. 13.
19 Although indicative of the NSL technique, Adams and Munro were atypical in that most of the League speakers concentrated on audiences away from the campus.

but unremunerated appearance. McElroy was the only one of the NSL historians who received a fee for his lectures, probably because his executive position created greater demands for his services.

NSL advertising preceded lecturers into the selected communities, describing their professional credentials and preparing an appropriate atmosphere. The following circular was typical of the advance blurbs:

> Dr. Van Tyne will discuss the antagonistic ideals of autocracy and democracy and will show how history has proven that the two cannot endure side by side. . . . The Pan-Germanic dream will be explained, and the educational scheme by which the German soul has been perverted. . . . the true foundations of German frightfulness, which is the Prussian theory of a state with no moral obligations, will be shown. . . . Dr. Van Tyne has been speaking before audiences all over the country, spreading the message of Americanism. He has spoken to over 70,000 people in the last four or five months.[20]

This promise of aggressiveness and attack proved the right combination for audiences in Van Tyne's region. He received far more invitations that he could honor despite a traveling schedule that would have taxed a much younger man.[21] During one tour that included Elgin, Joliet, Springfield, Urbana, Chicago, Indianapolis, Cincinnati, Canton, Zanesville, and Akron, he swung hard at the enemy and praised American participation in the war. His audiences sent their "echoes of appreciation," indicating that he had gauged the situation correctly.[22] With ever-mounting invitations and commendatory letters swelling his files, it is little wonder that the NSL lectures exhilarated Van Tyne and his colleagues.

The NBHS also organized a cadre of historian-speakers but took a less active role in scheduling lecture tours than did the League. To several hundred historians the NBHS sent a questionnaire in April 1918 acknowledging the increasing inquiries for scholars

---

[20] Advertising copy prepared for NSL circular, Box 1, Van Tyne Papers.

[21] Van Tyne was rare among the historians in admitting that he enjoyed these wartime duties.

[22] E. H. Krueger (Joliet Association of Commerce) to Van Tyne, 9 March 1918, Box 1, Van Tyne Papers.

qualified to speak on wartime subjects. The Board indicated that it wanted "to respond to such inquiries with definite suggestions as to lecturers."[23] Hence, the questionnaire asked historians whether they would be accessible for speaking, which topics they could prepare, and what sections of the country they would prefer. After compiling the answers into topical and geographical categories the Board placed advertisements in assorted magazines and journals regarding the "considerable number of the best known scholars and writers of history" who had offered their services.[24] As a kind of placement bureau, the NBHS merely filled requests and did not get involved in administrative or substantive details. One request, for example, came from the New York YMCA for a historian to speak on the causes of the war. The NBHS matched the appeal with information in its files and recommended that the YMCA contact William E. Dodd, who had indicated a preference for that topic and locality.[25] The tone and content of the talks belonged entirely to the historians and reflected little or nothing of NBHS philosophy about the war.

Closely related to this noncommittal role in supplying speakers was another project organized by the NBHS and one which the NSL actively supported. Chairman Evarts B. Greene had expressed a growing concern about America's failure to recognize fully other countries' contributions to the war effort. Once America entered the conflict, a tendency developed to forget the continuing role of the Allied nations and to overemphasize American importance. To counteract this sort of provincialism, Greene invited Professor George M. Wrong of the University of Toronto to visit several colleges in the United States and lecture on Canadian participation in the war. Both NBHS and NSL historians helped to arrange speaking and travel schedules for him and shared expenses of the tour.[26] Although the visit produced little national publicity, Wrong lectured to summer school students on the campuses of Harvard, Michigan, Indiana, Chicago, Northwestern, and Wisconsin, draw-

[23] NBHS Questionnaire, April 1918, Box 13, NBHS Records.
[24] *History Teacher's Magazine* 9 (June 1918): 303. This monthly magazine was closely associated with and partly financed by the American Historical Association.
[25] E. B. Greene to Guy V. Aldrich, 8 July 1918 (copy), Box 15, NBHS Records.
[26] Van Tyne to Greene, 21 May 1918, Box 8, NBHS Records.

ing attention to common ancestry, institutions, and ideals among the English-speaking peoples, and gently dispelling the speculations of an exclusively American victory.[27]

Advancing beyond speaker placement and goodwill tours, the NBHS created a series of illustrated lectures which reflected a discernible war rationale. This set of "lantern slides," accompanied by mimeographed lecture syllabi, encapsulated the thinking of NBHS historians in a medium that would retain its freshness no matter how frequently presented, and at the same time would preserve the original context. Jameson and a few members of the Board drew up six slide-lecture sets: "The Warring Countries and Their Geography," "The Growth of Germany and of German Ambitions," "The French Republic and What It Stands For," "The British Empire and What It Stands For," "How the War Came About and How It Developed," and "The American Democracy and the War." The scope and detail of the series revealed Jameson's wide interests, his continuing passion for accuracy, and his hope that the presentations would do something to help Americans "fight better and to make them more adequate citizens of the world afterward."[28] Each syllabus contained a full outline, cue lines for showing the proper slides, material for discussions, answers for anticipated questions, suggestions for parallel reading (primarily CPI pamphlets), and marginal comments to help the lecturer create an atmosphere conducive to persuasion. Even though they were meticulously conceived and packaged, these lectures allowed room for flexibility. According to the NBHS, the syllabi contained more material than a skillful lecturer could use, so "each lecturer is expected to use his own judgement in selecting, except that the set of slides provided will make it necssary for him not to ignore, entirely, any one of the chief topics."[29]

A random sampling from the six syllabi reveals the NBHS com-

27 Leland, "National Board for Historical Service," in Newton D. Mereness, ed., *American Historical Activities during the World War: Annual Report of the American Historical Association, 1919* (Washington, D. C., 1923), 1: 174.
28 J. F. Jameson to James Seth, 26 March 1918 (copy), Box 80, File 1514, Jameson Papers, Manuscript Division, Library of Congress.
29 Mimeographed lecture syllabi, Box 26, NBHS Records. This location is the source for all future references to the syllabi.

mitment to American participation in the war and its unique way of sharing this commitment with audiences. In the clear dichotomy of propaganda, the lectures first praised democracy, the Allies, and international law, and then condemned autocracy, the Central Powers, and unilateral diplomacy. Syllabus D, "The British Empire and What It Stands For," showed the positive approach. While a projectionist flashed on the screen a picture of David Lloyd George, the lecturer would paraphrase from the syllabus, "the prime minister, who has the real power, a Welsh schoolmaster's son, entirely a democrat," and explain how the Reform Acts of 1832 and 1867 had transformed England into almost "as much of a democracy as the United States." For a slide depicting American troops crossing Westminster Bridge toward the Parliament building, the lecturer's commentary related how American legislatures had used the British system as a model. Syllabus B, "The Growth of Germany and of German Ambitions," illustrated the unarguable Germanophobia of the series. In darkened tents or auditoriums, while slides of Bismarck, the Krupp munitions works, and a Zeppelin raid on England confronted audiences, the lecturer would attempt to

> make them see and know and feel sure that Germany, as at present managed, is really a serious danger to the rest of the world, and specifically to the U.S. To these ends it is necessary to show up the aggressiveness of Germany . . . her belief in force, her willingness to spend more than others in military and naval preparations, the unscrupulousness of her public conduct, the iron hardness of her rule—in a word, to show that she really was aspiring or tending toward dominating the world, and that domination of the world by her system would be intolerable.

If any doubts still lingered about how intolerable the system might be under Germany, Syllabus F attempted to remove those. Graphic scenes of the German army driving citizens of Louvain from their homes counterpointed an almost redundant description of "massacres and brutalities, destruction and plunder of villages and houses, devastation of farms and orchards," leaving little for the imagination.

By the end of the war, NBHS historians had presented these illustrated talks in twenty-two army training camps and had used YMCA and Knights of Columbus facilities for other appearances.[30] The correspondence files of the NBHS indicate that both audiences and historians enjoyed these shows and considered them good entertainment as much as propaganda. Demands for repeat engagements kept the Board busy replacing tattered syllabi and exhausted historians. So popular in fact did this visual-verbal propaganda become that some organizations attempted to borrow the NBHS equipment for private displays, and other groups, such as the Military Morale Section of the War Department, sought advice and assistance for creating its own series patterned after that of the historians.[31] Jameson remained somewhat reluctant, however, to allow the expensive set of slides to circulate too freely and he feared that the syllabi—no matter how carefully prepared— might be distorted when presented outside the control of "competent historical teachers."[32]

The CPI displayed less diffidence about its series of slide lectures, which were prepared with mass circulation in mind. These slides and lecture syllabi resembled the NBHS products in format but did not pretend to emulate the ideological content. The CPI series remained descriptive and inspirational rather than analytical and pedagogical. George Zook, professor of modern European history at Pennsylvania State College, designed many of the sets, the topics of which ranged from "Building a Bridge of Ships" to the extremely popular "The Ruined Churches of France." One lecture, "Our Boys in France," illustrated the essentially pictorial nature of the series as it showed "American troops in the front line trenches in France, in training in the great American cantonments abroad, on long hikes."[33] Sets contained an average of fifty slides each and cost approximately $7.50. By the end of the war

[30] Leland, "NBHS," p. 173.

[31] Leo Stock to Cornelia Pierce, 14 August 1918, and Stock to Jameson, 24 August 1918, Box 68, File 1206, Jameson Papers. Stock was one of Jameson's assistants at Carnegie and NBHS.

[32] Jameson to Lt. L. R. Fairall, Camp Dodge, Iowa, n.d. (copy), Box 68, File 1206, Jameson Papers.

[33] "Catalogue of Photographs and Stereopticon Slides," 9-A3, CPI Records.

the cpi had sold about 1,600 sets to schools, churches, and civic groups, which, unlike the nbhs lecturers, were free to supply whatever interpretation seemed appropriate.[34]

Individually and collectively, through sight and sound, the propagandizing historians of World War I seemed to confirm the theory that public speaking is a fickle art based largely on emotions and manipulation. Operating in an atmosphere charged with intense patriotism, fear, and hatred, they found that techniques which favorably impressed some audiences often antagonized others; oratorical chemistry applied as a catalyst produced uneven and unpredictable results. The nbhs discovered to its surpise that one of its projects—originally a modest one-man venture—turned out to be its most successful oratorical project of the war despite the fact that its content and style contained elements that could easily have backfired and created much unhappiness. By sending a historian on a goodwill trip to Great Britain the nbhs hoped to solidify Anglo-American relations but they could not have anticipated the unusual results or the even more unusual British response.

Academicians at the University of London had asked the nbhs in 1917 to send an American historian to speak at several English universities. A visit of this type, they said, would accomplish "a large amount of good by interpreting America to our people here, who are exceedingly anxious to know something about your intellectual position at first hand."[35] United States entry in the war in April 1917 had won unstinted appreciation from the Allies but three years of neutrality had raised doubts as to America's alignment with Allied ideals, especially following the war. America's aloof position since August 1914 and Wilson's vacillations and protests had created disappointment among the Allies that could not be forgotten even when American soldiers began to arrive in Europe. England needed to know that Uncle Sam and John Bull were close relatives, not temporary friends. Neither Creel nor

34 cpi, *Complete Report*, pp. 62-63.
35 Arthur Percival Newton to W. G. Leland, 15 November 1917 (copy), Box 3, nbhs Records.

Wilson favored the idea of sending extra civilians across hostile waters for such intangible goals and discouraged attempts to arrange any exchange programs of American and British professors.[36] Despite the lack of official sanction, the NBHS accepted the invitation and turned it into an American project rather than a mutual exchange between the two countries.

The project became known as the Mission among NBHS organizers and assumed the character of an apologia of America's role rather than an apology for tardiness. They wanted to affirm Anglo-American kinship while stopping short of obsequious filial piety. Leland handled most of the preparations and pointed out that "we do not want anyone to tell the English that the general feeling in America is that the Revolution was all a terrible mistake."[37] They wanted for this mission a scholar who could defend the traditions and posture of the United States and at the same time facilitate a rapprochement between the average citizens; in short, they needed a professional historian who was also "public-spirited, kind-hearted, and one of the most likeable of men."[38] The NBHS persuaded the University of Chicago that Professor Andrew C. McLaughlin would be an ideal envoy and obtained his academic leave for spring 1918.

The choice was a happy one. A friendly midwesterner from recent immigrant stock in Illinois, McLaughlin enjoyed referring to himself as a Scottish son of the Middle Border. Like many Americans he had opposed American involvement in the war but when involvement came he supported mobilization. His CPI pamphlet, *From Spectator to Participant*, had reflected this by weighing the horrors of war against the irresponsibility of shirking international duty. He also typified the average American's acceptance of German guilt for the war; his speeches for the NBHS and his University of Chicago pamphlet, *Sixteen Causes of the War*, delineated this verdict in unequivocal terms. McLaughlin's

---

[36] George Creel to Woodrow Wilson, 18 February 1918, and Wilson to Creel, 20 February 1918, Box 1, George Creel Papers, Manuscript Division, Library of Congress.

[37] W. G. Leland to C. H. Van Tyne, 9 February 1918 (copy), Box 9, NBHS Records.

[38] J. F. Jameson to James Seth, 26 March 1918 (copy), Box 80, File 1514, Jameson Papers.

presidency of the American Historical Association in 1914 had indicated his position of esteem within the profession, and his activities rivaled in prestige those of his good friend Jameson. He had formerly taught at the University of Michigan before becoming chairman of the department at Chicago, had edited the *American Historical Review,* and had been director of historical research at the Carnegie Institution. His monographs on American constitutional history revealed scholarly competence and his authorship of two textbooks displayed a broad knowledge of Anglo-American relations, all strengthening his credentials as a spokesman for the American position during the war.[39] McLaughlin also fulfilled the requirement of being "likeable." His reputation at Chicago was that of being clear-headed and big-hearted, and students as well as colleagues referred to him affectionately as "Andy Mac."

Not all historians, however, approved the NBHS choice of Mc-Laughlin. The NSL found much fault with his lack of support for the Allies prior to 1917 and considered him an odd choice to send abroad. Van Tyne and McLaughlin had long been friends and had coauthored a public school history text but found themselves sharply divided in 1914 at the outbreak of European war. While Van Tyne excoriated LaFollette, hyphenates, and pacifists in the press, McLaughlin tried to explain to his old friend the correctness of his unaggressive stand: "I am such a confirmed pacifist that I am willing that this country should lose its last dollar and its last man to beat the Kaiser, . . . in order that the world may be decent and respectable and not subjected to the horrible atrocities of war. . . . If this does not indicate a spirit of radical pacifism, I don't know what does."[40] Unconvinced by these explanations, Van Tyne awaited proof of McLaughlin's patriotism before withdrawing his opposition to the NBHS mission. Apparenly McLaughlin's speeches, pamphlets, and subsequent correspondence in early 1918 provided enough evidence and Van Tyne wrote the NBHS that his friend was "all right now" with

---

[39] See by McLaughlin: *The Confederation and the Constitution, 1783-1789* (New York, 1905); *The Courts, the Constitution and Parties* (Chicago, 1912); *A History of the American Nation* (New York, 1899); and *A History of the United States for Schools* (New York, 1911).

[40] McLaughlin to C. H. Van Tyne, 9 November 1917, Box 1, Van Tyne Papers.

his pacifism "burned and purged away."[41] Other NSL officials remained skeptical even longer and urged McLaughlin to suppress his objections to war and military readiness. Such ideas would supposedly undermine the American effort and the planning for continued preparedness after the war.[42]

Limited opposition such as that from the League did not deter McLaughlin and he went about preparing himself for the role of America's envoy. He had the NBHS staff compile a pamphlet of material for defending American honor and confirming that America was not only "doing its bit" in the war but doing it with enthusiasm. The pamphlet included lists of war legislation and taxes, numbers of drafted and volunteered soldiers, descriptions of patriotic and defense agencies, and amounts of war material being produced and shipped, all testifying to America's determination to win.[43] To assist him with the coordination of the burgeoning schedule McLaughlin had the benefit of Charles Moore, treasurer of the American Historical Association and chairman of the National Fine Arts Commission. The addition of Moore to the expedition was invaluable for he became an "official" liaison between the English and American historical professions and he kept systematic records of the trip, something McLaughlin found little time to do.

The scope of the mission expanded as the time for departure approached. Friends, relatives, and historians in America and Britain began to book additional speaking engagements for McLaughlin and arrange special dinners and social events. Jerome Greene, brother of the NBHS chairman, was attached to the Allied Maritime Transport Council in London and made contacts and accommodations outside the scholarly world.[44] As the scope grew, so did the expense, and only because public favor surrounded the mission did it succeed. The NBHS wanted the trip to be financially independent so McLaughlin would not feel responsible to or restricted by his British hosts, and the increasing commitments

41 Van Tyne to W. G. Leland, 13 February 1918, Box 9, NBHS Records.
42 Assorted correspondence, Box 3, Folder 2, McLaughlin Papers, University of Chicago Library.
43 Typewritten "English Tour" pamphlet, Box 9, NBHS Records.
44 Assorted correspondence, Box 3, Folder 2, McLaughlin Papers.

of the party jeopardized that independence. At one point the plans almost fell through for lack of funds, but Leland's tenacious appeals prompted enough private benefactors to finance the enlarged schedule.[45]

When McLaughlin and Moore sailed for England in late April 1918, the London *Times* heralded their objectives "to interpret the spirit of the Allies to the American people, and to expound to British audiences the history and future of Anglo-American relations."[46] Only partly known to the Americans at the time, the spirit of the Allies was at a low point now that Russia was removed from Germany's eastern front and Ludendorff was pushing through the west with his spring offensive. The two Americans were even less aware of how desperately the Allies needed the men and supplies aboard the convoy in which they rode. As the only civilian passengers among 1,500 soldiers aboard the troopship *Canopic*, they soon learned the immediacy of the war which lay before them. After an explosion which shook their vessel, Moore described the situation of April 26 in his datebook: "Going on deck we saw a destroyer racing between the lines of the convoy, a great bone in her teeth. . . . A German U-Boat had been discovered making for one of the convoy. A depth bomb fired at her periscope caused her to submerge."[47] After such a close encounter with the enemy and thirteen days at sea among eager untried "doughboys," McLaughlin landed at Liverpool much less a pacifist than before and prepared to give his audiences a taste of American fighting spirit.

Arriving in England as a part of the eagerly awaited American reinforcements, McLaughlin found his audiences ready to show their appreciation, and his two-month speaking tour received a gratifyingly warm response. By the end of his tour he had spoken before the Royal Historical Society, gatherings of teachers and workers, and more than twenty universities in England, Scotland, and Ireland. Four themes dominated his speeches: America's entry in the war, the background of American federalism, Anglo-American relations, and the current relevance of the Monroe

[45] Jameson to McLaughlin, 27 February 1918, in ibid.
[46] 24 April 1918, p. 5.
[47] Datebook, 1918, Box 1, and "Britain in Wartime" speech manuscript, Box 13, Charles Moore Papers, Manuscript Division, Library of Congress.

Doctrine. Under normal circumstances his English audiences could have enjoyed only the first of these. The others were serious —almost grim—reminders of British mistakes, America's new power, and the need of changing diplomacy after the war. If his British hosts had been expecting diplomatic overtures from their visitor, they must have been nonplussed, for the heart of McLaughlin's message more closely resembled an intellectual ultimatum.

The much-repeated speech on America's entry brought a predictably sympathetic response because it condemned Germany, praised British fortitude, and reiterated the idealism of the American declaration of war. It was basically the same speech that McLaughlin had delivered many times at home and that had appeared in part as a CPI pamphlet. With an explanation that was largely autobiographical, McLaughlin described how difficult it had been to convince Americans that they should enter the war: "It took the devastation of this horrible calamity, the death of millions, the crippling of tens of millions, the semi-starvation of a continent, the drowning of our own people, the slimy intrigue in our own nation, the practice of studied cruelty in Belgium and Poland—it needed all this to open our blind eyes; but at last we saw." And he evoked the memory of England's favorite American president, Abraham Lincoln: "The world cannot remain half free and half Prussian."[48] Following McLaughlin's first delivery of this address former Prime Minister Arthur Balfour said that it would "draw closer the intellectual, moral, and sympathetic bonds which already bound so closely together the two great nations."[49] McLaughlin appreciated the favorable response to his early speeches, not so much as a vote of confidence for his message but as a reassurance that his use of the language was acceptable. This applause quelled a previously unspoken fear and was "not without gratification to a son of the middle border brought up in a lumber town; if I can suit so nearly the standards of Oxford English, I think I'll manage to muddle through."[50]

Acceptance of McLaughlin's other speech topics required some

48 Andrew C. McLaughlin, *America and Britain* (New York, 1919), pp. 29, 33. This is a collection of his addresses delivered during the NBHS tour.

49 *Times* (London), 8 May 1918, p. 5.

50 McLaughlin to J. F. Jameson, 11 May 1918, Box 68, File 1206, Jameson Papers.

tolerance from a British audience. It seemed as if after delivering his prefunctory goodwill address at the beginning of the tour, he had settled in for a series of reprimands to the British, past and present. He admitted that America had caused some of the historic tensions with England but placed "the main burden for that hostility on Britain"; he argued that England's imperial aspirations had threatened to kill the federal system of separation of powers, and that the American Revolution had kept it alive by granting it permanent residence in the west[51]; and he urged the British to incorporate more American history into their schools in recognition of America's growth and England's decline as world powers.[52] Despite its pride in welcoming home a distant relative, the *Glasgow News* looked askance at McLaughlin's suggestion to orient the British history curriculum more toward America. The editors brushed off the plan as just another example of American blitheness and stated that "happy is the land that has no history."[53]

Few of McLaughlin's goading remarks received a rebuke more strenuous than that from the Glasgow editors, not even his recommendation that the rest of the world accept the Monroe Doctrine as the basis for future diplomacy. Other American historians had previously suggested this extension of American protection to democratic peoples and had not been very favorably received.[54] Europeans had listened coolly to these suggestions because they resented the implication of their need for American protection and they feared an America strong enough to impose its foreign policy upon other nations. McLaughlin renewed the proposal and hammered away with the benefits of a world stabilization of the geographical and ideological status quo. He described how President Roosevelt had greatly expanded the original intentions of the Monroe Doctrine, and hoped that its scope could be further broadened into a universal code to guarantee international peace

---

[51] McLaughlin, *America and Britain*, pp. 45-46, 177.
[52] *Times* (London), 17 June 1918, p. 5.
[53] *Glasgow News*, 17 June 1918, clipping in 1918 Datebook, Box 1, Moore Papers.
[54] See for example: A. B. Hart, "Shall We Defend the Monroe Doctrine?" *North American Review* 202 (November 1915): 681-92; John Latane, "The Monroe Doctrine and the American Policy of Isolation in Relation to a Just and Durable Peace," *Annals of the American Academy of Political and Social Science* 72 (July 1917): 100-109.

and order.[55] The coolness that had greeted other advocates of this idea somehow turned into applause when McLaughlin reiterated the arguments.

His traveling companion had early sensed this warmth and receptiveness to McLaughlin's speeches, even his reproving ones. He wrote that "McLaughlin is making a triumphal progress. Everywhere large audiences who are most appreciative and demonstrative."[56] McLaughlin marveled at the enthusiasm which greeted him, yet did not understand why they lavished him with such uniform approval. Later he privately speculated that he could have gotten an ovation if he had stood in front of the audiences and ordered them to "spell after me the following word, emphasizing each letter, A M E R I C A , also this word, W I L S O N . . . . A person unable to lecture to them would be a goop."[57] An English observer intimated why the audiences were so appreciative in spite of the occasional chiding tone of the speeches: "It is most refreshing to hear anyone who is so thoroughly in earnest and who believes so strongly in the future of democracy. The conduct of the war by this country has weakened people's faith somewhat. . . . [McLaughlin] arrived at a most opportune moment when the help of America is gradually making itself felt in the front lines in France. This means everything at the present juncture."[58] Perhaps the response did come from gratitude. It also could have been a reaction from people as weary of platitudinous speeches as they were tired of fighting. And following close upon Wilson's campaign for his Fourteen Points and the League of Nations, McLaughlin's speeches could well have accrued much of the approval produced by the president's idealism.

Whatever the reasons for its success, the mission was a prime example of oratory's negative chemistry producing positive results. The only sour note in the entire tour came while the applause still rang in McLaughlin's ears and had nothing to do with his rhetorical technique. While returning to America he knew that somewhere on the sea his ship would pass another carrying his son into battle

---

55 McLaughlin, *America and Britain*, pp. 172-73.
56 Charles Moore to W. G. Leland, 29 May 1918, Box 9, NBHS Records.
57 McLaughlin to J. F. Jameson, 13 July 1918, Box 68, File 1206, Jameson Papers.
58 H. P. Biggar to W. G. Leland, 18 May 1918, Box 9, NBHS Records.

in France. The younger McLaughlin died at his gun in the Argonne, denying his father the glow of triumph which otherwise would have prevailed following his visit to the Allies.[59]

Another historian using similar techniques produced much different results. Robert M. McElroy discovered that when he reprimanded Midwestern Americans they reacted with anger and returned his abuse, reversing the response that had greeted McLaughlin. The NSL had questioned from the beginning whether the Midwest was supporting the war as fervently as were other parts of the nation. Well-founded or not, these queries cast doubt on the patriotism of an area which contained many German-American residents, an ethnic vulnerability compounded by the presence of active socialist movements among recent Central European immigrants. To test its loyalty McElroy embarked on a three-week tour, giving speeches in many cities, including St. Louis, Kansas City, Omaha, St. Paul, Chicago, and Madison. Upon his return he continued his practice of presenting reporters with good copy. "In this trip," he said, "I have known what it was to face vast audiences shot through and through with unmistakable signs of pro-German sympathies."[60] He did not specify which communities he had found pro-German, thus building suspense, but two days later he revealed the information. In a *New York Tribune* interview on April 17 he leveled charges against the University of Wisconsin in Madison.

McElroy could not have chosen a more volatile area for his accusation; Wisconsin and its university were sensitive about the large hyphenated population and slurs on their patriotism. Barely three months before his indictment, some faculty members in a display of defensive loyalty had published a protest against "utterances and actions of Senator Robert M. LaFollette which have given aid and comfort to the enemy."[61] McElroy's visit to Madison on Saturday, April 6, had coincided ironically with a Liberty Loan parade and his speech was only one of several that afternoon in the

[59] Moore, "Britain in Wartime," Box 13, Moore Papers.

[60] *Hartford* (Conn.) *Courant*, 15 April 1918.

[61] Reprinted in George C. Sellery, *Some Ferments at Wisconsin, 1901-1947: Memories and Reflections* (Madison, 1960), p. 7. Sellery was professor of history at Wisconsin and co-author of the faculty protest.

university's Stock Pavilion. The city appeared anxious to prove its patriotism; government buildings, stores, and theaters closed to encourage a turnout and the local newspaper threatened that "it will be conspicuous to remain out of the parade."[62]

McElroy pointed out in his speech that "this state has recently been on trial as to whether it is American or German," and complimented the citizens for electing Senator Irvine Lenroot, whom he considered "every inch an American." The *Wisconsin State Journal* carried a brief account of the speech and described the 10,000 Liberty Marchers who had defied a cold rain to parade and attend the public speaking.[63] Judging from published reports it would seem that the city and university hardly deserved the charge McElroy brought against them. From haste or suppression the newspapers did not report the episode which gave rise to McElroy's accusations. One spectator, Professor Carl Russell Fish, quickly realized the danger of the unreported event and related it to a colleague before it became a public controversy. He described how the speeches had lasted more than three hours in the unheated Stock Pavilion, and that not more than a hundred of the several thousand people who had crowded into the building remained for the end of the program. Only the mandatory attendance of university cadets kept the arena from being almost empty. During McElroy's long address the weary, rain-soaked cadets grew restless, "some of them clicking their muskets and others 'schishing' to keep them quiet. McElroy, naturally uneasy to see his speech was not 'getting over,' lost his temper, and said, 'By God, I believe you are traitors!' And to this position he stuck, stating, after the meeting, that he knew that at least 60 per cent of the students were actively disloyal." Fish recalled how he spent that evening trying to convince McElroy that he had evaluated the situation incorrectly, but to no avail. Hence, he concluded from the events that "a nation-wide campaign of education directed by a man with no better judgment is mighty apt to prove a boomerang."[64]

[62] *Wisconsin State Journal*, 6 April 1918, p. 1.

[63] Ibid., 7 April 1918, pp. 1, 2.

[64] Fish to A. B. Hart, 9 April 1918, reprinted in U. S., Congress, House, *National Security League: Hearings before a Special Committee of the House of Representatives*, 65 Cong., 3 sess. (Washington, D. C., 1918-1919), 7: 538-39 (hereafter cited as *NSL Hearings*).

When the formal accusation appeared on April 17, the episode did boomerang, whirling between Madison and the NSL offices in New York and encompassing a greater amount of publicity than McElroy might have wished. The facts in McElroy's interview generally agreed with those in Fish's letter, but the interpretation differed. McElroy described the noise and restlessness in the audience and how he decided to see if it was his fault or whether "it was the American point of view that these young men objected to." So, he leaned forward from the podium and said, "I think you're a bunch of damned traitors! Well, what do you think happened? A loud outcry of protest? A stampede to pull me down on the platform? A demand that I retract that affront to their university? . . . What happened was absolutely nothing. . . . then I thought I'd test them a little further. . . . So a little later I said: 'I've often wondered what it would be like to speak before a Prussian audience. I think I know now.' Still there was no protest." He concluded that the student conduct had been one of the most disgraceful things he had encountered.[65]

All parties responded quickly and emotionally. The student newspaper called the *New York Tribune* revelations "abominable lies" and asserted that McElroy had fabricated the incident after leaving the campus; within a week the faculty demanded a "full, explicit, and emphatic" redress; the NSL executive committee responded by adopting a resolution fully endorsing McElroy's account of his Midwestern tour.[66] Both McElroy and the university took intransigent stands. The cold and rainy April 6 ordeal had placed Madison's honor on the line and two of its citizens in the grave from exposure; compromise seemed out of the question. Debate raged for months, polarizing positions and needlessly inflating the issue. State and university officials published their account, relying on spectators' testimony that McElroy's insults to the students had been nonexistent or inaudible or much milder

---

[65] *New York Tribune*, 17 April 1918, p. 18.

[66] *Daily Cardinal*, reprinted in *NSL Hearings*, 29: 1996-97; University of Wisconsin Faculty Resolution, 24 April 1918, reprinted in *Wisconsin Alumni Magazine* 19 (July 1918): 213-14; NSL Resolution, 17 May 1918, reprinted in University of Wisconsin, *Report upon the Statements of Professor Robert McNutt McElroy and the Executive Committee of the National Security League Relating to the University of Wisconsin* (Madison, [1918]), p. 8.

than his newspaper interview indicated.[67] The audience's silence following his remarks apparently proved its guilt to McElroy, and although he had been misquoted on some details, he did not withdraw his charge or apologize.[68] The university closed its case by refusing to allow any further representative of the NSL to speak on the campus.

McElroy and the NSL were subjected to severe criticism by historians for their inflexible actions. Other organizations and individuals continued to ferret out disloyalty but many looked with disdain upon the manner in which the NSL had handled this incident. Professor Fish had intended to join the League's summer education campaign until the affair convinced him that unless McElroy changed his tactics or relinquished leadership to "somewhat saner heads" he would have nothing to do with the program.[69] Frederick L. Paxson reflected this attitude. Even though his university was involved, he lamented McElroy's loss of control more than the test of loyalty. "Patriotic education in America needs courage and devotion," he wrote, "but it also requires truth and insight. These last, at least, were lacking on this occasion." Through an undisciplined approach McElroy's patriotism had become a "willingness to libel."[70] Public and private discussion of the event found historians once again aligning in their traditional camps: NSL versus CPI-NBHS. Hart and Van Tyne—already on record for pointing the accusing finger at disloyal groups—chose not to inflame the issue. Van Tyne attempted almost nothing in public defense of his NSL associate, confining his efforts to a series of private letters in which he tried to mollify McElroy's critics.[71] Ford confided to his wife that this event confirmed his suspicion, formed during other conflicts with the NSL, that McElroy was more foolish than he had earlier been given credit for.[72]

[67] University of Wisconsin, *Report*; George Sellery of the history department helped edit this report.

[68] McElroy testimony, *NSL Hearings*, 29: 1989-91.

[69] Fish to A. B. Hart, 9 April 1918, reprinted in *NSL Hearings*, 7: 538-39.

[70] Paxson, "The McElroy Affair," *Wisconsin Alumni Magazine* 19 (June 1918): 187-88.

[71] Paxson to C. H. Van Tyne, 26 April, 3 May 1918, Box 1, Van Tyne Papers. The letters from Van Tyne to which Paxson was responding are not available, but his arguments are repeated and discussed in Paxson's replies.

[72] G. S. Ford to wife, 8 June 1918, Folder 165, Ford Papers.

Oratory as a propagandist's tool proved a transient thing which historians during the war found effective if unpredictable. When they sought to assist, arouse, and inform with prepared speeches, slide lectures, or speakers' handbooks, the results were partly foreseeable and generally satisfying. When they attempted to persuade or intimidate, the results defied logic. Whereas McLaughlin's mission to Britain received intricate advance planning, McElroy's Midwestern tour grew almost spontaneously. And while no one attempted to predict audience response to McLaughlin's frequent scoldings, McElroy manipulated the publicity from his charges far beyond its worth. The different reactions to these two incidents pointed up the quicksilver quality of patriotic rhetoric and offered object lessons in oratory and advertising. The conduct of the historians involved in these and other oratorical ventures revealed more about their personalities than their scholarship, yet dramatized the fact that professional reputations are a combination of the two factors.

V. Historians as Censors

The editors of the *Atlantic Monthly* shared the fear felt by most authors and publishers in 1917 that wartime censorship would abridge the freedoms of expression guaranteed in the Bill of Rights. They consequently commissioned James Harvey Robinson to write an article delineating some of the problems involved in the suppression of ideas and information; this appeared in December 1917 and must have given the editors even more cause for fear. Robinson seemed resigned to the necessity if not the desirability of censorship. He explained that the exigencies of war could not always respect constitutional subleties and that America would have to accept these restrictions as part of the inevitable inequities of war. "When we start out to kill enemies on a broad scale, we are not likely to hesitate to gag those at home who seem directly or indirectly to sympathize with the foe." His acceptance of restrictions came more from a scale of priorities than from docility; the national crisis demanded sacrifices that transcended individual liberties. Censorship was strictly a transient measure and "need not be a serious cause of apprehension to any one," no matter how irritating.[1]

By the end of the war Robinson had reason to modify his blithe attitude and join others in lamenting the excesses of censorship. Criticism of his textbook *Medieval and Modern Times* (1916) for equivocation on German war guilt prompted the Justice Department to investigate his alleged pro-German sentiments and forced him to revise the text to avoid further attacks. With the aid of his Columbia friend Shotwell, whose patriotic credentials were beyond reproach, he rewrote portions of the recent chapters dealing with origins of the war and took a harder line on war causation. But even this compromise with anti-Germanism did not satisfy hyperactive critics; once accused, his loyalty remained suspect and his long friendship with Charles A. Beard compounded his supposed "disloyalty."[2] Theodore Roosevelt pronounced the revised text "an outrageous piece of German propaganda" that was "utterly unfit for use in American schools," and recommended that the National Security League investigate the matter.[3] In light of such publicity and criticism Robinson undertook another revision of his text which appeared after the armistice. In the three-year span between his first edition and the second revision, Robinson's appraisal of Germany traveled full circle. From a cautious division of war guilt among many belligerents he moved to a clear condemnation of Germany, a position more in line with the national temper.[4]

The zeal which characterized the Robinson affair is an example of the confusions in wartime censorship. Possessing an over-abundance of fear and protectiveness, patriots intimidated schools, libraries, and publishers with standards that they considered safe and proper. Attempting to smother the sounds of disloyalty in the folds of the American flag, they frequently entangled themselves in embarrassing episodes of intellectual shortsightedness. These self-appointed censors drew strength from federal leadership. Historians have since chronicled in detail the abuses which resulted from George Creel's press restrictions and from national legislation such as the Espionage, Sedition, and Trading with the Enemy acts. They have described the enthusiasm with which federal officials suppressed postal and political privileges for socialists, IWWS, suspected aliens, and other dissenters.[5] Official censorship and prosecutions, although deemed necessary at the time, offered dangerous models for nonofficial suppression of divergent points of view. Volunteer agencies of censorship flourished throughout

1 "The Threatened Eclipse of Free Speech," *Atlantic Monthly* 120 (December 1917): 813, 818.

2 G. S. Ford to Willis M. West, 27 August 1918 (copy), 3-A1, Tray 8, CPI Records.

3 Roosevelt to William W. Potter, 4 November 1918, in Elting E. Morison, ed., *The Letters of Theodore Roosevelt* (Cambridge, Mass., 1954), 8: 1389-90.

4 See the concluding chapters of Robinson, *Medieval and Modern Times* (New York, 1916, 1919).

5 See H. C. Peterson and Gilbert C. Fite, *Opponents of War, 1917-1918* (Madison, 1957); Donald Johnson, *The Challenge to American Freedoms: World War I and the Rise of the American Civil Liberties Union* (Lexington, Ky., 1963); Zechariah Chafee, Jr., *Freedom of Speech* (New York, 1920); James R. Mock, *Censorship, 1917* (Princeton, 1941).

the war and could hardly be expected to exhibit more wisdom or less intolerance than the government.

Creel had affirmed in April 1917, upon his appointment as CPI director, that "expression not suppression" would characterize the work of his organization. As it turned out, historians in the CPI as well as in the NSL and NBHS used both methods to obtain the desired results. Whether by expressing preference for an item or by suppressing a disfavored one they were able to determine the success or failure of much wartime communication. Approaching censorship in a piecemeal fashion these historians attacked each incident as a separate problem regardless of whether their actions were consistent with others taken within their organization or whether they contradicted those taken by one of the other organizations. As *ad hoc* censors they suppressed material they regarded as dangerous to national security and sanctioned other material by singling it out for publicity and wider acceptance. By either method their actions required that they sit in judgment on the acceptability of specific information for the American public.

The manner in which the NSL and the CPI handled the question of the German language reveals their divergent attitudes and procedures. Hundreds of public schools and colleges in 1917 offered German in their language curricula, and in some areas of predominantly German-American population, classroom instruction for all subjects in German was common. It was possible to find schools in such cities as Cincinnati and Milwaukee and in some areas of the Dakotas using German exclusively in their classes no matter if some of the students were not of German parentage.[6] The NSL joined other patriotic groups which felt that the use of the German language in America was tantamount to giving aid and comfort to the enemy. McElroy expressed the official NSL policy when he described the teaching of German in the public schools "as a harboring place for German propaganda," and Earl Sperry testified before a Senate subcommittee that German language instruction was dangerous to American unity and should be dropped from

[6] Carol S. Gruber, "Mars and Minerva: World War One and the American Academic Man" (Ph.D. dissertation, Columbia University, 1968), p. 21; Clifton J. Child, *The German-American in Politics, 1914-1917* (Madison, 1939), p. 7.

grammar schools and deemphasized on higher levels.[7] Although the United States commissioner of education opposed this campaign of suppression the League contacted teachers in New York and published appeals to teachers elsewhere urging them to discontinue instruction of German. Responding to a variety of such suggestions and pressures many schools agreed to do this and the NSL announced in July 1918 that schools in twenty-five states had dropped German from their program.[8] Deriving obvious satisfaction from these statistics, the NSL exaggerated its own role as a catalyst, but the results, from whatever motive, were real. By the end of the war and for many years thereafter schools were reluctant to use the language, and at least ten states passed legislation prohibiting its use in tax-supported institutions.[9]

McElroy also brought the strength of the NSL to battle against the "equally potent educational forces," the German-American newspapers, because they too by using German were "oiling the wheels for the German war chariot."[10] In this same battle Earl Sperry had for some time been investigating and fighting German-American newspapers, which he classified as a medium of subversion not unlike the tentacles of an octopus, a simile he incorporated in the title of his popular NSL pamphlet. The League aligned itself with other like-minded organizations and stretched the limits of the Sedition Act to threaten the foreign language press into relative silence. By applying pressure on advertisers and newsdealers the NSL claimed to have sharply curtailed the number and circulation of German papers in America.[11] Again, clear causation cannot be determined, but the number of German language periodicals and papers in America during the war years declined from about 500 to approximately 350, indicating that

[7] Robert McElroy, *Annual Report upon the Educational Work of the National Security League* (New York, 1918), pp. 28-29; U. S., Congress, Senate, *National German-American Alliance: Hearings before the Subcommittee of the Committee on the Judiciary*, 65 Cong., 2 sess. (Washington, D. C., 1918), p. 590.

[8] *New York Times*, 22 July 1918, p. 7.

[9] Mock, *Censorship*, p. 32; Lewis Paul Todd, *Wartime Relations of the Federal Government and the Public Schools, 1917-18* (New York, 1945), pp. 72-73.

[10] Variations of this argument appear in many McElroy utterances. See for example: *NSL Bulletin*, November 1918, and *New York Times*, 10 November 1918, sec. 1, p. 19.

[11] *NSL Bulletin*, September 1918, n.p.

the NSL historians were championing a popular and successful campaign of literary suppression.[12]

CPI historians, like those in the NSL, suspected that some German language classes had been serving as channels for German propaganda, but rather than cut off the channels they decided to fill them with American propaganda. Ford continued to argue the Wilsonian dichotomy that war involved nations and ideologies, not peoples and languages. To purge a language from America represented an act of blind provincialism and might further alienate once loyal German-Americans. He maintained that skillful use of their language in government propaganda could possibly help to insure their allegiance to America and enlist their aid in the war effort. Ford and Harding therefore supervised the translating and printing of the more popular CPI pamphlets in German and urged educators to use them in language classes to replace traditional German texts.[13]

German-American newspapers likewise received a more sympathetic treatment from the CPI than from the NSL. Working on the assumption that the foreign language press would reveal much about public opinion among nationality groups, the CPI commissioned historians to read local foreign language papers and report their findings to the CPI. Bernadotte E. Schmitt read and reported from the Cleveland area, as did William E. Lingelbach from Philadelphia, George Sabine from Missouri, and Solon J. Buck from Minnesota. A report from Lawrence Larson of the University of Illinois typified the nature of their revelations: "German-American editors are falling over themselves to get into the front ranks of loyalty. The editor of the *Peoria Sonne* is grieved to find that he must suppress his feelings, but he does suppress them."[14] Apparently the censorship work of other organizations and the natural pressures of wartime had largely silenced most of the dissent from foreign language presses, leaving little for the CPI to learn from them. Even though docile loyalty was preferable to dissent,

---

[12] *Century* 99 (March 1920): 636-38.

[13] Harding to Ford, 5 October 1917, 3-A1, Tray 4, CPI Records; Ford to John Finley (state superintendent of schools, Albany, N. Y.), 25 October 1917 (copy), in ibid., Tray 6.

[14] Larson to Ford, 9 November 1917, 3-A3, Tray 1, CPI Records.

Ford proposed a program of infiltration into the ranks of German journalism so that an active Americanism could replace mere passive acquiescence among hyphenated editors.[15] Little if any action transpired along these lines but the proposal does indicate the nonpunitive attitude which Ford held toward foreign language groups. Espionage and exploitation are not ennobling designs by any measure; but when gauged on the wartime spectrum with other means of controlling the foreign language papers, they do rank on the positive side of the scale.

The attitudes of historians toward history textbooks revealed more unanimity than was shown with the language problem. Historians generally left overt censorship of existing texts to private groups and individuals, including state defense councils, school-boards, vigilant librarians, and the War Department's Index Expurgatorius, which attempted to keep questionable literature off military bases. They frequently entered into controversies, however, such as the one concerning James Harvey Robinson, either because of personal friendships with the principals or because they were asked to arbitrate in disputes between publishers and groups hostile to particular books. Ford believed that publishers caused much of the controversy. He suspected that book companies were impugning the patriotism of authors being published by their competitors and drawing attention to cases of supposed pro-Germanism within their rival textbooks, all in an effort to gain greater circulation for their own products. His government position made him a much-sought-after arbiter and after trying to settle several conflicts and growing weary of the effort, he recommended that some sort of commission handle the problem of banned books and maligned authors.[16] Harding's presence in the CPI office added a touch of irony to the textbook problems. Only two years before, prior to American entry in the war, one of his highschool texts had come under attack from the National German-American Alliance because of its supposed anti-German bias, a twist of circumstances from which Ford could draw comic solace.[17]

[15] Ford to Larson, 25 July 1917, Box 1, Larson Papers, University of Illinois Library.

[16] G. S. Ford to George Creel, 24 August 1918, 3-A2, Tray 2, CPI Records.

[17] U. S., Senate, *Hearings, National German-American Alliance*, pp. 619-20.

Charles Altschul, an Anglophilic businessman, did much to focus historians' attention on the textbook situation. Shortly after the European war began the New York entrepreneur became distressed over the slowness of Americans to lend moral and military support to England in the latter's fight with Germany. He surmised that this reluctance sprang from decades of anti-English prejudices in public schools and textbooks. Convincing James T. Shotwell that the problem needed investigation and publicity, he and one of Shotwell's students, Harry Elmer Barnes, undertook a survey of approximately 100 school textbooks that were still in use across the nation or had been used in the past generation. The results of the survey confirmed Altschul's suspicions and appeared in the spring of 1917 in a small book entitled *The American Revolution in our School Textbooks*.[18] The booklet pointed up the need for rewriting texts to reemphasize the common heritage shared by the English-speaking peoples. It also allowed Shotwell to remind historians in a brief preface what a powerful effect they had on public opinion through their writing and teaching.

In line with these suggestions both the NSL and the CPI attempted to produce texts acceptable for wartime study. George H. Putnam, publisher friend of the NSL, compiled suggestions for a new text which would eliminate old prejudices concerning the American Revolution and draw clearer distinctions between representative government and Prussian autocracy.[19] So eager was the CPI to obtain an approved textbook for circulation in foreign countries that Ford commissioned Carl Becker to write one which would place heavy emphasis on democracy's relation to free land, equality, education, and self-government. Entitled *The United States: An Experiment in Democracy*, each chapter was an elementary essay showing Europeans how America had achieved over the years the things that Europe had wanted but had been unable to obtain because of its ingrained aristocratic traditions. The chapter on the American Revolution, for instance, placed less

---

[18] Barnes to author, 13 April 1968. Altschul later contributed heavily to the NBHS mission to Britain.

[19] As was the case with many similar propaganda undertakings, the work on this project stopped with the November Armistice.

stress on Anglo-American conflicts than on Becker's already well-known thesis of the internal revolution of the common men seeking self-government. And the brief review of government structure described the checks and balances which would prevent any tyrannical usurpation of power. The war ended before Becker finished the manuscript but Ford convinced Harper and Brothers to publish it and it appeared in 1920, too late to produce any significant impact as propaganda. Years later Ford reminisced that the Germans spoiled some very good enterprises by ending the war when they did, for he considered the book "one of the best introductions that any foreigner could read about American life."[20]

Perhaps the most memorable episode of literature suppression involving historians concerned the book *Two Thousand Questions and Answers about the War.* What began as a private reprimand by the cpi grew into a public condemnation by the nsl and ended as a rancorous debate among historians, journalists, and congressmen. The book was a catechism of war information published by the Review of Reviews Company, an American publishing firm managed by Albert Shaw and Charles D. Lanier. Lanier had been impressed with a semimonthly feature of questions and answers carried in an Australian periodical, *Stead's Review.* From a combination of patriotic and financial motives he obtained permission to incorporate part of the material in a booklength version and arranged for a New York journalist to edit and supplement it for American readers.[21]

Shaw explained the project to George Creel and persuaded him to write an introduction to the volume. In his brief prefatory remarks Creel maintained that the war would not be won until "it dominates every thought and activity. This burning consciousness can be gained only through an exact knowledge of the facts in the case. . . . The '2000 Questions and Answers,' in my opinion, constitutes a vital part of the national defense." This rewritten and enlarged Australian dialogue went on sale in the spring of

---

[20] G. S. Ford, "Reminiscences," Columbia Oral History Collection, copy at University of Minnesota Library, 3: 551-52.

[21] Lanier to Creel, 24 September 1918, 1-A1, Tray 35, cpi Records.

1918, enhanced by Creel's introduction. The Review of Reviews sold 3,000 copies through its subscription service and arranged with the George H. Doran Company to publish a similar edition for commercial sales. The favorable response prompted a second edition, but before this could be implemented unexpected questions arose and found the publishers unable to supply answers as readily as their catechism had done.

Ford obtained an early copy of the book and immediately perceived that Creel's usual impetuosity had involved him in a difficult situation. Ford wrote to his CPI superior in tones reminiscent of a professor scolding a careless student. "I take it for granted that you did not see the text of the book before you wrote the introduction," he said, and explained that the book appeared to be "a pacifist half pro-German affair." He doubted that the publishers had intentionally created this appearance, but even if they had not the book was still "about the poorest excuse that I have ever seen with its general 50-50 attitude on responsibility for the war, its entire omission of anything that straightout condemns the Germans." To protect the CPI he suggested that Creel protest to the Review of Reviews about the inclusion of his introduction in such questionable material.[22]

Aware that his introduction had given indirect government sanction to the book, Creel paraphrased Ford's letter, added a few comments about the book's "evasive, straddling note," and sent the protest to Shaw, asking to be consulted before the printing of a second edition.[23] The following week Ford supplemented Creel's letter with a seven-page critique of the portions of the book that he considered objectionable. In this critique Ford pointed out that neither he nor the CPI possessed a "war neurosis" or "perverted patriotism" which would cause them to suppress disagreeable opinions. Yet as a historian, educator, and government official he could not refrain from inquiring about certain aspects of *Two Thousand Questions and Answers*, particularly since "this is the type of book that will be eagerly seized by teachers." Ford said that he had consulted with three other his-

22 Ford to Creel, 25 June 1918 (copy), in ibid., 3-A2, Tray 2.
23 Creel to Shaw, 26 June 1918 (copy), in ibid., 1-A1, Tray 35.

torians whose opinions he respected in an attempt to dispel or verify his own doubts, and they agreed that the book was sympathetic to Germany.[24]

Ford criticized the book specifically for emphasizing British control of the seas as a contributory cause of the war, and for describing pan-Germanism, British imperialism, and French chauvinism as similar concepts. He argued that discussions of Britain's Boer War and naval construction gave the impression that they were as sinister as Germany's quest for a "place in the sun" and U-boat warfare. He objected to the favorable presentation of German education and political franchise and to the failure to treat in greater detail Zeppelin warfare, German war practices in Belgium, and the historic militarism of the Junkers. And he cited many examples of phraseology, organization, and use of statistics designed so that "the average reader will get an incorrect impression out of actualities." Reaffirming that he was not an official censor, Ford left the decision to the Review of Reviews as to what should be done about the book. But he concluded his attack with the ominous understatement that "I can hardly regard with equanimity the extensive distribution of this book."[25]

The Review of Reviews accepted this criticism with surprising grace. Shaw explained that most of Ford's objections applied to those passages which had originally appeared in *Stead's Review*. He speculated that the British editor had been "so extremely anxious to be judicial-minded that like a good many liberal Englishmen, he was unduly critical of his own Government." These sections had been written at an earlier date for a British audience and the American editor had been mistaken in temperament rather than disloyal when he allowed them to pass on to American readers. The editors would use more exacting standards in revising the book, Shaw promised, so that no equivocations would remain in the material.[26] This acquiescence to cpi wishes approached subservience. The Review of Reviews withdrew orders for a second

24 Ford to Shaw, 3 July 1918 (copy), in ibid., 3-A1, Tray 9.
25 Ibid.
26 Shaw to Ford, 8 July 1918, in ibid., 1-A1, Tray 35.

printing and asked Ford to recommend someone to supervise the revision along lines suitable to the CPI. Ford referred them to Shotwell, who in turn referred them to Carlton J. H. Hayes (Columbia) and J. Salwyn Schapiro (City College of New York). These two historians—primarily the latter—offered suggestions for change and by early September the revised edition neared completion. The editors had brought it up to date, created a more sympathetic tone toward the Allies, and included a section on German atrocities, all of which would improve its chances of acceptability.[27]

Had the episode ended there it would hardly be worthy of consideration. The chain of events had been private, good-natured, and without reprisals. The censorship, such as it was, involved voluntary cessation of a second printing followed by revision under supervision of two historians. But just as the episode seemed to be reaching a happy end it exploded with bitterness and publicity. Unknown to Ford or the Review of Reviews other forces were planning their own recourse against the book while it underwent revision. William H. Allen, director of the Institute for Public Service in New York City, had sent out distress signals in several directions including the White House and the NSL concerning the evils of the book. The NSL referred him to Van Tyne, who reviewed with him portions of the book and concurred about the "seriousness of the errors of history and pro-German leaning."[28] Once alerted to the situation the NSL decided to use it as an object lesson and devoted a large part of the League staff to the cause.

A telephone call from the NSL to the Review of Reviews on September 1 gave a preview of the forthcoming imbroglio. According to Lanier, an NSL publicity director called him with the announcement that Professor Van Tyne was preparing a denunciation of *Two Thousand Questions and Answers* and invited him to submit a statement which would be published with it. Lanier made a hasty trip to the NSL offices where he and Van Tyne succeeded only in trading insults.[29] Compounding the frustration

27 Lanier to Ford, 9 July, 5 September 1918, in ibid., 3-A1, Tray 9.
28 Allen to Joseph Tumulty, 10 September 1918, in ibid., 1-A1, Tray 35.
29 Lanier to Creel, 24 September 1918, in ibid., Tray 35.

of this new threat to the book was the irony that Albert Shaw, president of the Review of Reviews, had only recently been appointed to the advisory committee of the NSL.[30] Despite the irony of the situation and the interview with Van Tyne, Lanier did prepare a statement setting forth the history of the affair, hoping that its publicaion would counteract the damage which he feared from the denunciation.

Van Tyne's critique confirmed those fears. Distributed to the press on September 11 without Lanier's counterstatement, the NSL denunciation arraigned both the Review of Reviews and George Creel. Van Tyne called the book "a masterpiece of pro-German propaganda. The German Government could not have devised anything more insidious, more calculated to destroy our faith in our allies, and to insinuate into the American mind excuses for Germany. . . . a subtle vein of disparagement of the high principles for which the allies fight runs through it all." He listed twenty-eight examples of "disloyal and subtly pernicious" information and questioned whether Creel was a safe man to occupy the directorship of the government's publicity bureau.[31] For many years Van Tyne's friends had recognized his ability to wither an opponent with a barrage of criticism. To avoid what one historian called his "verbal gatling" they generally sidestepped issues on which they knew Van Tyne to be sensitive or inflexible.[32] In this instance the passions of war seem to have unlimbered his equipment for a field day at the firing line.

Newspapers filled columns the next few days with excerpts from the book and its denunciation, refutations of both, and editorials which cast blame in all directions. Creel presented his defense in an open letter to the NSL in which he reprinted his June 26 protest to Shaw. He complained that there had been no need for the NSL to publicize a book which had been removed from circula-

[30] Lawrence F. Abbot to Shaw, 16 January 1918, NSL Folder, Albert Shaw Papers, New York Public Library.

[31] Van Tyne, NSL publicity release, reprinted in U. S., *Congressional Record*, 65 Cong., 2 sess., pp. 10380-81. Abridged and paraphrased versions of the denunciation appeared in several newspapers on 11 and 12 September, but the most convenient place to study the complete version is in this reprint of 17 September.

[32] W. G. Leland to Van Tyne, 12 August 1915, Box 1, Van Tyne Papers, Michigan Historical Collection, Rackham Building, University of Michigan.

tion two months previously, and suggested that Van Tyne's "sense of honor is somewhat subordinated to his weakness for a little cheap notoriety."[33] Lanier seconded this charge and protested that Van Tyne had not only taken great liberties when quoting from the book, but that the NSL had not printed the Review of Review's statement as it had promised.[34] Other newspapers agreed; the *New York American* branded the NSL crusade against the book "small and contemptible."[35] The NSL replied that the revision of the book had not been publicized sufficiently to counteract the damage done by the first edition already in circulation. Hence the League felt obliged to dramatize the issue in an effort to ward off its effects.[36] Van Tyne continued his attack. He said that Creel could not be absolved for writing the introduction and that he must have been dishonest, unscholarly, or blind not to see the "poison of Prussianism" which pervaded the book.[37] Senator Henry Cabot Lodge echoed these sentiments in Congress but added a heavy swipe at censorship in general.[38] Deciding that all parties shared the guilt, the *New York Times* called the book "seditious," Creel's introduction "careless," and Van Tyne's critique "not fair," and wished a plague on all their houses.[39] The Review of Reviews published a drastically revised version of its catechism after the invective had cooled, having suffered the consequences of being kind to Germans. Creel also learned to be more circumspect about writing introductions for unread manuscripts. The two historians most directly involved, Ford and Van Tyne, emerged from the episode in strikingly different condition.

Ford's criticism had been harsh but discreet. His actions had arisen from a desire to protect the CPI as much as to suppress a questionable book. He had singled out the material which he found offensive and suggested historians who might undertake revisions. The Review of Reviews responded to his criticism in the manner in which it was offered and dutifully began to rectify

33 *New York Times*, 13 September 1918, p. 13.
34 Ibid.
35 16 September 1918, editorial page.
36 *New York Times*, 14 September 1918, p. 9.
37 *Christian Science Monitor*, 14 September 1918, p. 7.
38 U. S., *Congressional Record*, 65 Cong., 2 sess., p. 10378.
39 14 September 1918, p. 10.

the situation. The entire process had taken place without publicity or recriminations. Ten years later hardly any of the material which Ford objected to would have aroused much concern among historians. Most of the offensive ideas became standard interpretations as time, fuller information, and revisionist historians divided the war guilt among the belligerents and gradually softened the indictment of Germany. When viewed in the milieu of 1918, Ford's actions can almost be justified. As an official publicist for a nation at war with Germany, he could hardly have allowed *Two Thousand Questions and Answers* to pass. The balancing of evidence by the editors appeared at the time to be sympathy for Germany and condemnation of the Allies. Working with an admitted patriotic bias, Ford suggested that the book could participate in more worthwhile calisthenics than bending over backwards to be fair to the enemy. His attitude lacked objectivity, but considering the circumstances it was understandable. His methods were commendable in light of the many intimidations that other censors employed.

Van Tyne's criticisms of the book were almost identical with Ford's. He objected to the relativist tone which did not openly oppose Germany and praise the Allies, and many of the passages which he found objectionable were the same ones that Ford had pointed out. Other than this common ground of substantive matter Van Tyne's censorship activity had almost no similarity to that of Ford. The methods he employed during this brief episode gave rise to questions concerning his ethics as a scholar and widened the breach between cpi and nsl historians. The strident tone of his denunciation helped create an atmosphere of intolerance and gave credence to Lanier's claim that he had been unable to reason with the Michigan professor. Apart from his polemical style, the manner in which Van Tyne presented the examples of pro-Germanism in the book also cast doubt on either his honesty or his editorial competence. In attempting to show how twenty-eight of the questions and answers were "pernicious," he often distorted the material. When questioned about some of his more obvious misquotations and distortions Van Tyne admitted that there had been some technical difficulty printing the extracts he had chosen from the book. Hence, proof sheets of his denunciation had failed to indicate ellipses where he had deleted phrases from quotations. Printers partly remedied this in the final version by inserting asterisks whenever possible; nevertheless, some quotations emerged in garbled form.[40]

The interpolations, selection of material, and editorial comments which Van Tyne used often forced innocent material into his mold of pro-Germanism. The following excerpts from the original *Two Thousand Questions and Answers* juxaposed with Van Tyne's version in the NSL denunciation typify his method and show the resulting problem.

ORIGINAL TEXT	VAN TYNE'S VERSION
Q. Has Germany a Constitution?	Q. Has Germany a Constitution?
A. Yes; it has a written constitution, which is, on the whole, similar to the constitution of most large nations, defining and limiting the power of the Government and directing the general method of making laws and enforcing laws. It went into effect on April 16, 1871.	A. Yes; it has a written constitution, which is, on the whole, similar to the constitution of most large nations. (Could anybody but a bigoted pro-German make such an answer?)[41]
Q. Is the German Parliament at all like the United States Congress?	Q. Is the German Parliament at all like the United States Congress?
A. In some ways it is like Congress. . . . The	A. [same answer, followed by] Damnable deceit! Note the purposeful con-

40 Ibid., p. 9.
41 Review of Reviews, *Two Thousand Questions and Answers about the War* (New York, 1918), p. 216; U. S., *Congressional Record*, 65 Cong., 2 sess., p. 10380.

Bundesrat, or upper house, on the other hand, represents not the people of Germany but the States specifically, as our Senate was supposed to do when United States Senators were selected by State legislatures. . . .

fusion of the principles and spirit of the two institutions. The German upper house is, of course, made up of members appointed by the sovereigns of the German states. Our Senate never was chosen by such autocratic method.[42]

It is difficult to justify Van Tyne's editorial standards even with allowance for wartime patriotism. *The Nation* showed him no mercy. It deplored this censorship attempt which blackened "the reputation of Professor Van Tyne as a scholar and his honor as a man,"[43] and one newspaper condemned his actions as "morally not a bit better than forgery."[44] Van Tyne reacted to this abuse in a manner which for him was unpredictably diplomatic: he retreated into relative silence. Within a few weeks armistice came and brought with it enough balm to take the sting from episodes such as this. Van Tyne's personal papers reflect this same human impulse to suppress unpleasantness; the only mention of the affair in his collected correspondence from the war years is a small number of letters from obscure individuals praising his stand. One of his colleagues summed up the event in a bittersweet mixture of compassion and condemnation:

Van Tyne of Michigan was and is a fine scholar. Only the war and certain interests he was developing when the war began have upset his good judgment. It has been known to many of us sometime that his balance was no longer maintained when England and the war were discussed. . . . It is a pity that instructors of the young and those who have charge of teaching history should be weak enough or passionate enough to do what Van Tyne has done.[45]

[42] Ibid.
[43] 107 (21 September 1918): 312-13.
[44] *New York American*, 16 September 1918, editorial page.
[45] W. E. Dodd to George Creel, 20 September 1918, 1-A1, Tray 35, cpi Records.

An incident involving the NBHS historians in censorship activity raised similar questions about professional conduct and contributed to a historical debate that is still unresolved. Rather than attempt to suppress or discredit material the NBHS endeavored to lend credibility to a set of propaganda documents by giving them its scholarly sanction. The Board's function was to approve instead of condemn so that the subject of its attention might win wider acceptance. The documents in question were a curious assortment of German and Russian correspondence which purported to prove that the Bolshevik regime was a puppet government controlled by the German general staff. The tortured convolutions which characterized the Bolshevik revolution and the Brest-Litovsk Treaty had switched Russia from the Allied camp to that of Germany and had forced America to revise much of its thinking and propaganda. This diplomatic somersault left the CPI publicists with a paucity of explanations until the advent of these clandestine documents offered an opportunity to describe the situation as further evidence of Germany's duplicity and proof of its plans for world domination.

Edgar Sisson, a former editor of *Cosmopolitan Magazine*, had obtained the documents in March 1918 while serving as CPI representative in Russia. An anti-Bolshevik journalist in Petrograd had informed Sisson of secret papers in government offices which would discredit the Soviets. Intrigued by this information, Sisson established a liaison with other sympathetic agents who, during the confusion which surrounded the government's transfer from Petrograd to Moscow, managed to steal, photograph, or make copies of the documents. Sisson returned to Washington with his cache of goods, convinced that they would be more than worth the money and chicanery required to obtain them.[46] The Department of State took a less sanguine attitude. It hesitated to publicize the "Sisson Documents," doubting their authenticity and fearing adverse diplomatic effects in Russia. But Sisson and Creel convinced President Wilson that they were "absolutely conclusive" proof of Lenin's and Trotsky's collaboration with the

[46] Edgar Sisson, *One Hundred Red Days: A Personal Chronicle of the Bolshevik Revolution* (New Haven, 1931), pp. 357-58; George Kennan, "The Sisson Documents," *Journal of Modern History* 28 (June 1956): 130-31.

German government. They exposed an "amazing record of double dealing and corruption" that would constitute a coup for American propaganda.[47]

Wilson consented to CPI wishes and allowed the documents to be made public despite misgivings from his Department of State. Not the least of his reasons for this action may have been that American military intervention in Russia taking place during the summer of 1918 caused many Americans to doubt the sincerity of the president's former statements about nonaggression and self-determination. Used effectively these documents would help to reinforce the government's current anti-Bolshevik policy and remove some of the contradiction that separated Wilsonian rhetoric from military policy. Hence, government officials subjected the documents to a series of tests to guarantee their authenticity. The CPI was satisfied by September 15 that the documents had been verified and edited sufficiently, and issued them in daily installments to the press.

Reaction to the first installments did prove the CPI revelations a coup but one of doubtful effect. Whereas the *New York Times* accepted the documents' authenticity and called the Bolsheviks despicable "German valets,"[48] other sources found the information suspicious. The *New York Evening Post* charged publicly what had heretofore only been rumored—that many of the documents had been published previously in European papers and had been generally discredited. The editors wondered, in fact, whether Sisson and the CPI weren't the victims of a "gigantic hoax."[49] Shortly the head of the Finnish Information Bureau called the documents "brazen forgeries" which Russian counterrevolutionaries had channeled to Sisson to discredit the Bolsheviks.[50] Princeton historian and CPI aide Edwin S. Corwin intervened in this debate by pointing out that although the documents might be authentic their credibility needed to be established.[51]

47 George Creel to Wilson, 9 May 1918, Box 2, Creel Papers, Manuscript Division, Library of Congress.
48 16 September 1918, p. 10.
49 16 September 1918, scrapbook clipping, 17-D1, Tray 4, CPI Records.
50 *New York Times*, 22 September 1918, p. 10.
51 *New York Evening Post*, 4 October 1918, scrapbook clipping, 17-D1, Tray 2, CPI Records.

Creel discussed the situation with Ford, and in consideration of the growing criticism of the documents, asked the NBHS to appoint a committee to examine them. He suggested that a group of historians review the charges that had been made and if the verdict was favorable to the CPI, the documents and the NBHS report would be issued in pamphlet form.[52] The NBHS immediately appointed Jameson to head the investigation and acquired for his assistance Samuel N. Harper, professor of Russian language and institutions at the University of Chicago. Although other historians and language specialists such as Archibald Coolidge received requests to aid in the project, the pressure of time and conflicting assignments left Jameson and Harper to conduct the examination largely by themselves. For the next two weeks these two men labored to clear the Sisson Documents of their forgery charges.

Despite impressive credentials and good reputations, both men were odd choices to serve on the committee. Jameson knew little Russian and could not read most of the documents. Neither did his varied career include much experience with Slavic or Central European affairs. He described his position as that of "vulgar ignorance"; he nevertheless undertook the task with ardor.[53] If Harper possessed more relevant credentials than Jameson, he was admittedly not an impartial judge. The son of the University of Chicago's first president, he had become one of the first Americans to make Slavic studies a full-time scholarly pursuit and had been teaching at his father's school since 1905. During his frequent trips to Russia he had established friendly contacts with liberal groups who were trying to reform the czarist government, and while accompanying the Root Mission in 1917 witnessed the first revolution which gave control to a new provisional government. After he returned to the United States, he grew increasingly disillusioned with the chances for liberal reform as the Bolsheviks assumed power and withdrew Russia from the war. Even before being selected to help with the NBHS investigation he had become

[52] George Creel to Joseph Schaefer (NBHS vice-chairman), 18 October 1918, Box 31, NBHS Records.

[53] J. F. Jameson to A. C. McLaughlin, 30 October 1918 (copy), Box 63, File 1081, Jameson Papers, Manuscript Division, Library of Congress.

an outspoken foe of the Soviet regime and had committed himself in print to a defense of the documents' authenticity.[54]

With Creel pressing for a swift and favorable verdict and Harper having to return to his campus duties in a few days, the two historians proceeded to examine and evaluate the documents. Jameson later recalled to a colleague, "It was a good seminary exercise, and seemed to us relatively not a difficult one. . . . [We] subjected them to all the tests that you or other members of the profession would naturally think of."[55] Harper translated the documents, then they compared the text materials with known facts, questioned Sisson about their acquisition, received some technical advice from government experts, and tried to answer the questions that had arisen since the first publication of the series. Five days after beginning the investigation, Jameson reported a generally favorable verdict to the NBHS executive council.[56] Samuel Harding and the CPI printers immediately began resetting the documents into pamphlet format while Jameson wrote the NBHS report using Harper's notes and a frantic postal exchange of proofsheets, revisions, and suggestions between Washington and Chicago.[57] The combined report and documents, entitled *The German-Bolshevik Conspiracy*, appeared just days before the armistice.

The 2,300-word report offered respectability to the documents; it vouched for their authenticity, answered the criticism that had greeted the CPI newspaper versions, and explained in layman's terms how and why the NBHS historians arrived at the verdict. Of the sixty-eight documents examined, fifty-three were originals or photographs and the committee decided that they had "no reason to doubt the genuineness or authenticity of these fifty-three documents."[58] The remaining documents were copies or translations and the two historians reserved judgment on them because of in-

54 *Christian Science Monitor*, 26 September 1918, p. 5.

55 Jameson to Arthur I. Andrews, 24 January 1919 (copy), Box 9, File 102, Jameson Papers.

56 Paul V. Harper, ed., *The Russia I Believe In: The Memoirs of Samuel N. Harper, 1902-1941* (Chicago, 1945), pp. 111-12; minutes of the NBHS executive council meeting, 24 October 1918, Box 25, NBHS Records.

57 Jameson to Harper, 28 October, 5 November 1918, Cabinet 3, Drawer 4, and Cabinet 1, Drawer 1, Samuel N. Harper Papers, University of Chicago Library; Harper to Jameson, 30 October 1918, Box 31, NBHS Records.

58 CPI, War Information Series, no. 20 (Washington, D. C., 1918), p. 29.

sufficient evidence. Although they did not believe them forgeries, they did not feel qualified to pronounce them genuine and relegated them to an appendix in the pamphlet because of their questionable status. This appendix group of documents was the object of most of the early criticism according to the report. Some of them had been discounted by European papers prior to their CPI release, and their faulty translations, minor internal contradictions, and confusing dates did provide ground for doubt. But in view of more detailed investigation and the authenticity of the fifty-three originals, Jameson and Harper felt the criticism either fell away or did not offer substantial reason to discredit the bulk of the collection.

The NBHS report ventured no opinion on the interpretation which Sisson and the CPI had drawn from the documents; it verified only their physical reliability. This distinction was apparently too subtle for most readers, however, for the impression prevailed that the NBHS historians agreed that Lenin and Trotsky were paid agents of Germany and that the Bolshevik government was only a puppet regime for the unspeakable Hun. Although Jameson was unsure about this interpretation and Harper opposed it, the inclusion of their report in the pamphlet with the documents made them partners by association.[59] One recent historian who has criticized the government's use of the document to bolster its military policy has also criticized the historians for not speaking out plainly enough on what their NBHS report was saying. Their silence, "although it may have satisfied their consciences, was bound to be interpreted as an endorsement of the Sisson thesis."[60] Jameson soon realized that their discreet silence was interpreted as acceptance of the "conspiracy" theory and resigned himself "to pay the penalty of our caution."[61]

The Nation, which seemed to be the self-appointed conscience of historical integrity, meted out the penalty by labeling the NBHS's work a "sham investigation" and calling for a "stern rebuke from

[59] Harper to Ford, 15 November 1918, 3-A1, Tray 22, CPI Records.

[60] Christopher Lasch, *American Liberals and the Russian Revolution* (New York, 1962), p. 115.

[61] Jameson to Arthur I. Andrews, 24 January 1919 (copy), Box 9, File 102, Jameson Papers.

every American historical scholar who values the good name of his profession."[62] The editors described Harper as a paid attorney for anti-Soviet forces and lamented Jameson's complicity in the affair. They asked, "Must the reputation of American scholars go by the board as a part of the wreckage of war?" Jameson had no fears about his reputation and stuck by his original verdict in the report. He confided to an acquaintance, "As for what *The Nation* said about Sam Harper and me, I should worry. I take the liberty to believe that our reputation for honest and careful statement stands higher than that of *The Nation*. . . . As old Cromwell said, 'I know not why they should not as well be at our mercy as we at theirs.' "[63]

Harper was neither as secure nor as insouciant as Jameson and he fretted for some time about the event. His Chicago colleagues, McLaughlin and Dodd, reassured him that the sniping letters and journalistic barbs were little cause for worry; still his misgivings prevailed and his correspondence with Jameson displayed a growing self-flagellation about the whole affair.[64] The Department of State conducted an inconclusive review of the episode in 1920 which uncovered little proof but did raise more doubts about Sisson, the documents, and some of Harper's conclusions in the report.[65] Later in his memoirs Harper recalled his unhappiness about the use of the NBHS report to sanction an interpretation of which he disapproved. He had wanted to include in the report a statement that the Bolsheviks would have withdrawn from the war for their own motives; and that whether they were German agents was immaterial and dubious at best. The CPI discouraged this, however, because such a statement would make a weaker impact than the less ambiguous Sisson interpretation.[66] In the unpublished original draft of his memoirs Harper continued that this experience "showed clearly the pressure to which University men are subjected in time of war. . . . Thanks to the support of

---

[62] 107 (23 November 1918): 616-67.

[63] Jameson to C. H. Van Tyne, 3 December 1918 (copy), Box 86, File 1678, Jameson Papers.

[64] Harper to Jameson, 27 November 1918, Box 31, NBHS Records.

[65] "Sisson File," Cabinet 3, Drawer 4, Harper Papers.

[66] Harper, *The Russia I Believe In*, p. 112.

Professor Jameson I was able to hold out to a certain degree against a complete abandonment of the rules of the student but it was impossible for a University man not to make a contribution to the development of the war spirit, even if this involved the making of statements of a distinctly biased character."[67]

These wartime pressures produced more than bias. That two historians, neither with proper credentials for the task, should grant their sanction to these documents was questionable from the outset. To offer this sanction after less than a week's investigation with knowledge of the unreliable quality of some of the documents, and under CPI pressure to conform their verdict to the Sisson interpretation, was a suspension of judgment. More recent research has confirmed that the NBHS report, in addition to its other indiscretions, was probably wrong. The historian-diplomat George F. Kennan debunks both the Sisson documents and the report in an examination of handwriting, language, letterheads, seals, typewriter analysis, dating systems, logic, and historical fact. He pronounces the documents forgeries and wonders "how the American experts could have arrived at such a judgment."[68]

The answer to this question is obvious but not convincing enough to justify their actions. In their attempt to approve material for propaganda purposes Jameson and Harper became involved in the same type of censorship situation facing Ford and Van Tyne in the *Two Thousand Questions and Answers* problem. They all succumbed to the pressures of national bias and placed war aims above scholarly restraint. Whether they used "expression or suppression" in their censorship, these historians departed from historical standards and discovered, unhappily, that the influence of their activity was insignificant to the war effort. Compared to their pamphleteering and public speaking, the censorship work required more time on smaller projects, influenced

[67] Unpublished memoirs draft, Cabinet 3, Drawer 4, Harper Papers.

[68] Kennan, "Sisson Documents," p. 143. For concurring analysis see: Z. A. B. Zeman, ed., *Germany and the Revolution in Russia: Documents from the Archives of the German Foreign Ministry* (London, 1958), p. x; Lasch, *American Liberals,* pp. 113-17; Peter G. Filene, *Americans and the Soviet Experiment, 1917-1933* (Cambridge, Mass., 1967), pp. 47-48.

fewer people on less important issues, and created more problems of a professional nature. The reluctance with which they undertook censorship chores testified to their academic reserve, but the results, whether futile or not, remained one of the less savory aspects of their propaganda work.

VI. In & Out of the Classroom

When Guy Stanton Ford addressed the National Education Association convention in 1919 his appearance belied the tone of his remarks. The high stiff collar accentuated the darkness of his tight-fitting suit and the graying hair and prim glasses created an aura of wisdom and academic respectability. But his speech more closely resembled that of an athletic coach congratulating a victorious team than that of a university dean and history professor. He told the assembly of educators that the most amazing thing about America's participation in the war was that "the final victory was won . . . by the silent triumphs of an army of teachers in the schoolrooms."[1] Had these remarks been merely vacuous they could easily be forgotten; instead they were a distortion of reality, a fact he and his audience fully realized. Teachers had failed to make their classrooms an effective agent of wartime patriotic instruction and Ford's postwar effusions could not alter that fact. His CPI files were filled with correspondence from frustrated teachers who were unable to handle war issues in their classrooms. Confessions such as "confused and overwhelmed," and "scarcely know what to do" were typical of their attitude. Professor S. H. Clark of the University of Chicago visited schools from New York to California during the war and complained to George Creel that "not one school in twenty was doing anything like effective work."[2]

Part of the classroom's failure as a propaganda medium came from the decentralization of America's educational system. The diversity of state and local school administration in 1917-1918 doomed efforts to coordinate or standardize instruction in a nationwide campaign. Six months after America's entry in the war the CPI could not obtain the names and addresses of all local superintendents of education, and as late as autumn of 1918 a complete list of the nation's schools and teachers was still unavailable.[3] Then there was the problem of the Great War's timing. When war came to America in April 1917, less than two months remained in the school year, making it impossible to inaugurate a meaningful program of instruction until the following September. Likewise, the armistice in November 1918 disrupted schedules by making newly devised war-oriented courses obsolete.

Lack of clear purpose compounded the problem. The war found American schools just as unprepared to integrate education with war as it had found the military and industrial mechanisms unready to support mobilization. The plethora of zealous private and local organizations that bombarded educators with suggestions and demands did more to hinder than to help the development of successful teaching. Typical of these disruptions was the request for students to join in victory and loyalty demonstrations. Long lines of singing and marching school children became *de rigueur* for patriotic observances during the early months of the war, and frequently these public displays constituted the only instruction available on war issues. One superintendent reported that his students had participated constantly in civic programs until their education was suffering. "I have had to make enemies," he continued, "by refusing to parade my children at every demand."[4] The lack of unanimity among teachers as to what their responsibilities were during the crisis also prevented concerted efforts in many areas. The Illinois superintendent of public instruction described the confusion in his state that had resulted from conflicting and overlapping programs, producing more annoyance than patriotism.[5] By the time schools had achieved a semblance of order and purpose, the war was almost over.

Ford's unrealistic appraisal of this triumphant army of teachers could well have come from his embarrassment with the part played by historians. Early efforts by the CPI, NBHS, and NSL to use classrooms for propaganda were unsystematic and half-hearted. Not

[1] "The Schools as They Have Affected Government Activities," *National Educational Association: Addresses and Proceedings of the Fifty-seventh Annual Meeting, 1919*, p. 539.

[2] S. H. Clark to Creel, 23 March 1918, 3-A1, Tray 6, CPI Records.

[3] Lewis Paul Todd, *Wartime Relations of the Federal Government and the Public Schools, 1917-18* (New York, 1945), p. 36.

[4] E. B. Tucker (Helena, Ark.) to CPI, 23 May 1918, 3-A7, Tray 2, CPI Records.

[5] Francis G. Blair to CPI, 22 May 1918, in ibid.

until many months had passed did any of the organizations produce a comprehensive program for schools. Their initial projects were unenthusiastic partly because most of the historians preferred to aim their propaganda at adult groups. They anticipated a short war and did not see the need of concentrating on the younger population which was only indirectly involved with mobilization. Even NSL Education Director McElroy admitted that working with teachers was his "second line" of operation,[6] and Ford remained unconvinced that his main responsibility was to indoctrinate youth. When Ford began his belated CPI programs for public schools they attempted in large measure to use teachers as channels for reaching parents instead of just instructing students.[7]

A brief review of some of the early projects for schools undertaken by the NBHS, CPI, and NSL illustrates their half-hearted interest in this segment of the population. The NBHS sponsored an essay contest for teachers on the topic "Why the United States is at War." One criterion for judging was the appeal which the essay would have for school children; hence, elementary and secondary teachers competed in separate divisions. State winners in both divisions received seventy-five-dollar prizes and then entered a national competition against other state finalists. While more than 600 teachers entered the contest, they represented only fourteen states, indicating that the project depended more on the energy and initiative of individual states and teachers than on the NBHS.[8] Ford displayed the same passive attitude concerning educators. Although he considered the CPI pamphlets pertinent educational material he made no real effort to have them distributed in schools. The CPI did advertise them in educational periodicals and mailed them to teachers on request; again, the initiative for their use remained with the teacher. The one pamphlet which would have been appropriate for use in elementary schools was a collection of patriotic songs and poetry called *The Battle Line of*

---

6 McElroy, "Patriotism: Past, Present and Future," *National Education Association: Addresses and Proceedings of the Fifty-sixth Annual Meeting, 1918*, p. 95.

7 Ford to Creel, 22 March 1918 (copy), 3-A2, Tray 1, CPI Records.

8 *New York Times*, 28 July 1917, p. 2; W. G. Leland, "National Board for Historical Service," in Newton D. Mereness, ed., *American Historical Activities during the World War: Annual Report of the American Historical Association, 1919* (Washington, D. C., 1923), p. 178.

Democracy. Its price of fifteen cents and its limited printing of 94,000 copies prohibited its widespread adoption in classrooms and showed that the CPI was not intending the pamphlet for mass distribution.[9]

McElroy's flair for drama produced a more active program in the first year of the American war effort than either the NBHS or the CPI developed, but the results were hardly more impressive. The NSL arranged a cooperative project between the Chicago and New York City boards of education in which teachers of the two school systems attended "Talks on Americanism" by exchange speakers. McElroy later estimated that more than 30,000 teachers participated in the program and heard speeches by professors from Columbia, the University of Chicago, and the NSL.[10] Auspicious in its numbers, the project offered little more than patriotic exhortations, and whatever benefits may have been gained by this exchange were probably canceled by another NSL campaign operating at the same time. Assuming the worst from suspected disloyal teachers, the NSL had from the start of the war urged school administrators to act vigilantly in "weeding out such members of their teaching force as are not enthusiastically supporting America's position in the war."[11]

By exhorting and purging simultaneously the NSL symbolized the early cross-purposes and unsystematic approaches that failed to take advantage of the patriotic potential of the nation's schools. As the war progressed historians realized that they need not be so concerned about the loyalty and enthusiasm of teachers. The lack of concrete suggestions for making classes more relevant to war issues constituted the real problem. This need for a revised curriculum, new perspective, and coordinated historical instruction in the schools soon began to occupy the talents of historians and in the latter months of the war they produced some ambitious educational programs which contained more propaganda than history. Whether the schools used these programs effectively or whether the students reacted more to the idealism or intolerance

[9] CPI, *Complete Report*, p. 15.

[10] *New York Times*, 10 March 1918, sec. 1, p. 16; McElroy, "Teaching Teachers," *Independent* 93 (30 March 1918): 525.

[11] NSL *Bulletin*, June 1918, n.p.

of the propaganda is impossible to determine. Admitting these imponderables, the primary consideration is that of the historians who produced the new approaches to wartime education, not the success or failure of their implementation.

The NBHS inaugurated its first comprehensive propaganda campaign for schools in the September 1917 issue of the *History Teacher's Magazine,* an adjunct of the American Historical Association. Here historians published four articles each month for nine months, suggesting ways to use history courses as vehicles for bringing the war into classrooms. The articles attempted to help teachers restructure their classes by infusing current war issues into the regular assignments and at the same time imparting the righteousness of the Allied cause. The series offered, according to its managing editor, "the common ground on which history and patriotism meet," and sought to bring historians, teachers, and students together as partners in the war effort.[12] The Board historians had waited six months to start this series, not so much from indifference to the problems of teachers as because they wanted a sustained program that would coincide with the regular school year. Evarts B. Greene organized the series, edited the articles on American history, and channeled the articles of other history fields through the chairmen of three more subcommittees: Johns Hopkins's Ralph V. D. Magoffin (ancient history), Princeton's Dana C. Munro (European history), and Michigan's Arthur L. Cross (English history). Each chairman recruited additional historians to write articles showing how their special areas could lend themselves to patriotic instruction. When the series ended in May 1918, more than twenty-five historians had contributed articles.

While the articles were in preparation during the summer of 1917, the U. S. Bureau of Education helped publicize the forthcoming series by circulating among educators a bulletin, *Opportunities for History Teachers.* This government publication called

---

[12] U. S., Bureau of Education, *Opportunities for History Teachers: The Lessons of the Great War in the Classroom,* Teachers' Leaflet, no. 1 (Washington, D. C., 1917), p. 3.

attention to the semiofficial status of the NBHS historians and gave the four chairmen a chance to preview some of the suggestions for reorienting history classes "in light of the Great War, especially since America itself has become one of the belligerent powers." Almost without exception the four men warned against using patriotic oversimplifications, while still stressing the necessity for emphasizing new interpretations to make both history and the war more meaningful.[13]

This attitude also characterized the preparation of the articles. The historians admitted that history classes presented a logical channel for patriotic education, yet at the same time they feared the abuse of history through chauvinism and wartime intolerance. Munro's position illustrated this intellectual dualism. He told Greene that "in the present emergency it seems clear to me that if the teacher cannot conscientiously and whole-heartedly lend his influence to supporting the war with Germany, . . . he ought at least to keep silent."[14] Still, he warned teachers that "there is danger lest in the enthusiasm for the new points of view, we should neglect the well-known and fundamental features, and either pervert or caricature the history of the past."[15] The almost inevitable result of this ambivalence was the cautious tone of the suggestions for teaching wartime history. From the thirty-six articles, as cautious as they were, emerged several themes which, if followed, would transform history classes into a handmaiden of propaganda. A sampling from each of he four areas exemplifies these themes and reveals the NBHS's new commitment to indoctrinating youth.

Professor James H. Breasted (Chicago) introduced the ancient history series with the suggestion that teachers could produce fruitful lessons by showing how the rise of a national state and the desire for conquest and empire in ancient Egypt paralleled the European imperial rivalries of the late nineteenth and early twentieth centuries. The interpretation he drew from the parallels

13 Ibid., p. 1.
14 D. C. Munro to E. B. Greene, 13 July 1917, Box 5, NBHS Records.
15 Munro, "Suggestions for the Course in Medieval History," *History Teacher's Magazine* 8 (September 1917): 217-18.

implied that America could consider itself proud not to have been enveloped in this "old and familiar cloak of a selfish and sordid nationalism."[16] William D. Gray (Smith) took Breasted's parallels forward to another age, showing how "ancient Caesarism and imperialism are living forces in Germany today." He compared Roman and German desires for conquest, the worship of power, the "pompous and arrogant speeches," and the "grandiose and brutal triumphal monuments," and concluded that German teachers taught their students "that it is their mission to take the place of Rome as he great conquering and civilizing power." Gray drew the same moral lesson from these parallels as did Breasted; he declared that the Germans lacked the old Latin *humanitas* and were probably more akin to barbaric Huns than to ancient Romans.[17]

While the ancient history series concentrated heavily on the use of historical comparisons to create unflattering portraits of the Central Powers, the European history series encouraged the introduction of new materials in classrooms. Munro's initial article defended the legitimacy of reinterpreting history to meet current needs and suggested that teachers should replace some of the old emphasis on Western Europe with consideration of the Balkans, the Mideast, Russia, and interrelations between Asia and Europe. Not until Americans understood these factors, he argued, could they understand the ethnological and commercial problems which had been so instrumental in bringing on the war.[18] Robert Kerner (Missouri) supplemented Munro's general suggestions by offering some new insights into the complexities of Eastern Europe. He explained that the Slavs had developed their defensive nature through centuries of being overrun by large nations in Europe and Asia, and that it was not by accident that these people now looked to America, France, and Britain for "fresh hope and practical assistance." Kerner praised the new Russian government, which had recently overthrown the czarist regime, for what it had contributed to the "democratization of world politics," little

16 Breasted, "Ancient History and the Modern World," in ibid., pp. 214-15.
17 Gray, "The Great War and Roman History," in ibid., 9 (March 1918): 138-39.
18 Munro, "Suggestions for Medieval History," pp. 217-18.

aware that within a few weeks the Bolshevik revolution would make his comments both obsolete and embarrassing. At the time, however, it seemed expedient to congratulate the progress made by America's new ally and to make its national characteristics palatable for school children.[19]

A predictable Anglo-American filial devotion permeated the English history articles. Chairman Cross had indicated in the Bureau of Education's publicity bulletin that his series would emphasize common heritage so that Americans could better appreciate "their origins in English soil, in order to labor the more intelligently and devotedly to preserve their existence."[20] Most of the articles followed this pattern, showing the cultural and historic ties that made the two nations more than mere military allies. Wallace Notestein reviewed seventeenth-century political development to illustrate the institutions that had embedded themselves in American government. He traced the origins of American political parties, parliamentary systems, and the executive cabinet to their English antecedents and stressed that these were central to democratic life.[21] Charles H. McIlwain (Princeton) displayed even more generosity in cultivating the family tree. He affirmed that America was the legal descendant of medieval England, "and the more careful the study of our institutional history becomes, the greater is likely to be our feeling of gratitude to the framers of the English Constitution."[22]

The American history series combined themes from the ancient and European history articles to create a composite approach; it drew parallels for instructive purposes and offered new interpretations for old courses. In this diversified manner Greene managed to get from his historians more concrete suggestions and aids for the teacher. At the same time, some of the American history articles adopted the exhortative quality found in the English history series. Carl L. Becker filled his essay on the Monroe

---

[19] Kerner, "The Historic Role of the Slavs," *History Teacher's Magazine* 8 (November 1917): 294-95.

[20] Bureau of Education, *Opportunities for History Teachers*, p. 16.

[21] Notestein, "The Interest of Seventeenth Century England for Students of American Institutions," *History Teacher's Magazine* 8 (December 1917): 350-51.

[22] McIlwain, "Medieval England," in ibid., 8 (October 1917): 257-58.

Doctrine with homey analogies and rhetorical questions. He argued that America could no longer use the doctrine in a Little Jack Horner manner to protect its geographical interests in an isolated corner of the world. Instead it must now be expanded to guarantee ideological interests. The war had become a struggle between democracy and autocracy transcending national boundaries and invalidating earlier interpretations of the doctrine. "Can it be supposed, then, that such a defeat for democracy in Europe would not be a menace to democracy in America?" He thus defended America's role in the war as a crusade to fight for its ideals on a world scale.[23]

In a tour de force of comparative analysis, Carl Russell Fish (Wisconsin) showed how current domestic mobilization matched that undertaken during the Civil War. He pointed out the common problems in the two wars involving transportation, military conscription, restrictions of the press, nationalization of resources, and suspension of some legal rights, and maintained that these could be regarded as tests of democracy's ability to survive. Stretching his parallel lines almost to the breaking point, he suggested that the Civil War struggle to emancipate American slaves presented an instructive object lesson when compared with the Allied desire to free Germany's conquests and vassal states.[24]

Greene had cautioned historians about the dangers of generalization, simplistic parallels, and arbitrary interpretations; all these pitfalls appeared during the nine-month run of the series, giving the chairman's warning a hollow ring and offering scholarly models for potentially dangerous practices. Although the magazine's average monthly printing of 3,000 copies increased to 10,000 when the series began, it is difficult to estimate the influence that the articles exerted on classroom instruction.[25] It would be presumptuous to assume that the influence increased at the same rate as the magazine's circulation and dubious to suggest that all history

[23] Becker, "The Monroe Doctrine and the War," in ibid., 9 (February 1918): 87-90.

[24] Fish, "Internal Problems during the Civil War," in ibid., 9 (April 1918): 199-200.

[25] Albert McKinley (editor, *History Teacher's Magazine*) to W. G. Leland, 14 September 1917, Box 5, NBHS Records.

teachers followed the guidelines literally. Shortly after the series ended Greene commented to an Illinois associate that the benefits of the project were doubtful. Much of the work he felt was "not very intelligently done and almost invariably the teacher finds it difficult to bring to the discussion of recent events anything approaching a just historical perspective."[26] Whether the series did more to inspire wartime patriotism in its young audience or to distort their understanding of world history is a moot point; the potentials and atmosphere for both were present in the nation's classrooms.

That the pitfalls of the series disturbed some historians appeared in the reaction of one of its participants. W. L. Westermann (Wisconsin) had agreed to contribute an article on the Roman Empire, then decided the dangers involved in the project overshadowed the anticipated gains. He wrote the chairman of the ancient history group, asked to be replaced by someone who agreed more fully with the aims of the series, and worried about the actions of his colleagues. "If they permit themselves to suggest to secondary teachers that they should make analogies and draw lessons from the past to stimulate patriotism or to explain the present war, they will have done a serious wrong. . . . They will have played into the hands of the pseudo-historians."[27] Despite misgivings, Westermann remained on the committee and his article appeared in the February 1918 issue. His contribution resembled the others in the series except for its greater hesitancy to impose patterns on historical events. Perhaps he decided after seeing the first articles that the effects were not as bad as he had feared, or perhaps his sense of civic duty overpowered his caution.

Whatever Westermann's reasons for remaining on the project, he and his associates produced a body of material that consciously attempted to manipulate the instruction of history for nonacademic ends. They used the resources of their craft to create a synthetic product and designed it to function for pragmatic and transient purposes. The restraint with which most of the

26 Greene to Lawrence Larson, 10 July 1918, Box 1, Larson Papers, University of Illinois Library.
27 Westermann to R. V. D. Magoffin, 10 July 1917 (copy), Box 5, NBHS Records.

historians executed their assignments did save the series from becoming a tragic commentary on wartime scholarship. Their suggestions, on the whole, were innocuous even if questionable, and the completed series received little criticism from teachers or historians. Jameson's early invitation for historians to counteract "unsound" information with their "sound" knowledge met with a rather loose interpretation in this instance, but the contributors stopped short of seriously embarrassing their profession.

During America's second year of participation in the war historians began to offer teachers a broader variety of assistance than in the opening months. While the NBHS series in the *History Teacher's Magazine* continued to be of some use in history classes, other phases of instruction came under their attention. By the time of the November armistice the NBHS, NSL, and CPI were deeply involved in many educational activities that they had hesitated to undertake previously. Their commitment to classroom propaganda increased as the war lengthened, and they made greater use of teachers as agents of patriotic instruction. War issues began to consume a greater part of the school day as intellectual mobilization lowered its age limits to include even the youngest students. Historians were largely responsible for replacing many of the children's flag-waving parades and lunchtime victory gardens with systematic programs of academic study.

As the CPI became more aware of the needs of civic education among school children, it transformed one of its military indoctrination projects into a syllabus for teachers. Ford and Harding had originally intended to organize an outlined study of the war for use in army training camps and now decided to expand its scope for civilian use. They asked the NBHS to assist in the project and with its cooperation Harding's *The Study of the Great War: A Topical Outline, with Extensive Quotations and Reading References* became one of the most comprehensive and popular study aids during the war. Appearing first as an NBHS supplement in the January 1918 *History Teacher's Magazine* and then in April as a CPI pamphlet, the outline reached a circulation of more than 700,000, with 40,000 extra copies of the *History Teacher's Magazine* version selling for twenty cents each.[28] When Ford called the outline "an exceptionally effective thing" he spoke as a propagandist rather than a historian, for Harding had designed the study as a medium of persuasion more than of instruction.[29] He divided the syllabus into ten topical outlines, appended a bibliography of suggested readings, and drew from these sources profuse quotations to support his outline headings and divisions. In format the study resembled the NSL's speaker handbooks except that its orientation was toward the classroom rather than the orator's platform.

Harding's syllabus purported to be a study of the war but was, in fact, a transparent argument for the Allied cause. By means of highly selective topics, skillful arrangement of evidence, and a minimum of editorial comment he presented an effective, albeit unbalanced, case. The first topic, "Fundamental Causes of the War," outlined the kaiser's arbitrary foreign policy and Germany's attempts for a "place in the sun," and cited such sources as Bernhardi, Nietzsche, and Treitschke to establish the militaristic character of the Germans. The third topic, "Indications that Germany and Austria Planned an Aggressive Stroke before June 28, 1914," left no doubt about the author's predilections and matched German documents and quotations with Entente sources to dramatize the difference in attitudes. Topic Six depicted the violation of Belgium and offered a standard review of "the burning, the shooting, the starving, and the robbing" which condemned the Germans beyond refutation. Most of the ten topics employed the popular techniques of juxtaposing quotations, allowing Germans to indict themselves, and arguing a point to a syllogistic conclusion while ignoring contradictory evidence.

The bibliographies added authority to the topical outlines by recommending publications with sympathetic views. Almost one-third of the sources that Harding listed were other CPI pamphlets. If this left much to be desired from a historian's standpoint, it succeeded in presenting an illusion of scholarship and in referring

[28] CPI, *Complete Report*, p. 16; Todd, *Wartime Relations*, p. 49.

[29] G. S. Ford to R. M. McElroy, 30 November 1917 (copy), 3-A1, Tray 2, CPI Records.

readers to literature considered safe. The collected diplomatic documents of the belligerents comprised another third of his listings. For the uninitiated these booklets could offer substantiation for almost any case; Harding supplied the proper guidelines and marshalled them into a phalanx of testimony favorable to the Allies. The remainder of the bibliography contained standard works, periodicals, and speeches. This list indicated that Harding possessed as much skill in compiling acceptable literature as in organizing argumentative outlines. The two parts of the pamphlet complimented each other and presented a more complete arsenal for teachers to use in their classes. Intended for use in secondary schools, the syllabus found ready acceptance in college classes as well. The first copies appeared early enough for several second-semester study groups to organize, centered around the ten topics and readings.[30]

Following closely upon Harding's syllabus came Wallace Note-stein's NBHS study-guide for the new Student Army Training Corps (SATC). The fall semester of 1918 would see more than 500 American colleges and universities participating in this cooperative venture with the War Department, and one of the required classes for the 125,000 student-soldiers was the war issues course.[31] National director for this course was Frank Aydelotte, an English professor from Massachusetts Institute of Technology, who appealed to the NBHS for assistance in drawing up a guideline for the schools to follow. Dana Munro and Joseph Schaefer, the new chairman and vice-chairman of the Board, helped Notestein cull 40,000 questions that the War Department listed as being frequently asked in army camps. From these they chose 112, answered them by supplying brief bibliographies relevant to the topics, and published the collection as a pamphlet, *Questions on the Issues of the War*.[32] Most of the questions dealt with predictable topics: Prussian militarism, the status of Alsace-Lorraine,

[30] Frank J. Klingberg (University of California, Los Angeles) to G. S. Ford, 29 January 1918, 3-A1, Tray 5, CPI Records.

[31] Frank Aydelotte, *Final Report of the Students Army Training Corps*, (Washington, D. C.: War Department, Committee on Education and Special Training, 1919), p. 7.

[32] Reprinted in ibid., p. 14.

and German atrocities, and the suggested readings were standard sources available at most colleges, supplemented by CPI pamphlets and Harding's syllabus. Employing this pamphlet as a common denominator, the various colleges devised war issues courses (sometimes called war aims courses) to suit their special needs. A few chose historians to direct their classes, such as Claude H. Van Tyne at Michigan, Evarts B. Greene at Illinois, August Krey at Minnesota, and Andrew McLaughlin at Chicago, but many more delegated the task to professors from other disciplines.[33]

Language, art, science, and technology specialists all contributed their energies and prejudices to the courses and the result was interdisciplinary instruction at its best and worst. The dean of Lafayette College commented during the program that "it will not be strange if the student goes out from the War Aims Course in possession of a knowledge which savors a little too much of 'clothes line gossip' about a hated neighbor rather than of the substantial facts of history."[34] NBHS historians had already grown disenchanted with the way the SATC had departed from Notestein's guidelines and developed into quasi-history, and few lamented its rapid demobilization following the November armistice. Aydelotte got a quick rebuff when he approached the NBHS with plans for publishing a book of some material from the war issues courses. Vice-chairman Schaefer told him that "it is time to get back in our teaching to as nearly 'scientific' or 'historical' or 'philosophical' a spirit as is possible to us. Such books as the one here planned would simply tend to perpetuate an attitude of mental aberration."[35]

While CPI-NBHS historians concentrated on syllabi and guidelines for students and soldiers in the final months of war, the NSL implemented another of its oral campaigns. McElroy organized a cadre of his regular NSL historians—A. B. Hart, Thomas Moran,

---

[33] Carol S. Gruber, "Mars and Minerva: World War One and the American Academic Man" (Ph.D. dissertation, Columbia University, 1968), p. 296; Leland, "NBHS," p. 177.

[34] Albert K. Heckel, "The War Aims Course in the Colleges," *Historical Outlook* 10 (January 1919): 20-22.

[35] Joseph Schaefer to Frank Aydelotte, 21 December 1918 (copy), Box 15, NBHS Records.

Earl E. Sperry, Claude H. Van Tyne—and several other professors to visit summer school classes of teachers' colleges and conduct sessions on civic education. Naming this program "Teachers' Plattsburg" after the volunteer civilian military encampments, McElroy predicted that those who participated in the sessions would become "an army organized and mobilized to interpret truth and to destroy ignorance."[36] With his usual verve he attracted publicity and wide interest for the project. The editor of the *Journal of Education*, completely taken by the siege mentality which characterized the planning, praised the forthcoming class-room maneuvers as an unprecedented battle in the service of democracy and humanity.[37]

"Teachers' Plattsburg" turned out to be a series of isolated skirmishes instead of a unified campaign, but its activity was not without importance. The NSL coordinators visited more than 250 summer schools in forty-three states and conducted sessions that lasted from a few days to several weeks in length. Stressing patriotism and the eradication of foreign influences, they helped teachers develop Americanization programs geared to their local communities and classroom conditions. McElroy estimated that at the end of the campaign they had distributed approximately twenty-eight tons of printed material to supplement the oral sessions and had contacted 300,000 teachers.[38] One feature of the NSL summer school sessions which distinguished them from other campaigns was the attention given to Negro colleges, institutions not generally publicized during the war effort. Patriotic workshops in Negro colleges in Virginia, North Carolina, Alabama, and Texas were prominent in McElroy's planning, and Dr. Lewis B. Moore, dean of Howard University, organized special adult education classes in Negro communities in Louisiana and Mississippi under the NSL aegis.[39]

Although no single example can represent the NSL technique, Van Tyne's sessions at the University of Virginia illustrate one

36 *New York Times*, 17 June 1918, p. 13; McElroy, "Teaching Teachers," p. 525.
37 *Journal of Education* 87 (6 June 1918): 630.
38 McElroy, *Annual Report upon the Educational Work of the National Security League* (New York, 1918), pp. 21-23.
39 *NSL Bulletin*, September 1918, n.p.

approach. During his three days at Charlottesville he lectured to audiences exceeding 2,000, often conducting the meetings out of doors on the steps of Mr. Jefferson's classic rotunda; following the lectures he carried on an extensive correspondence with teachers relating to the suggestions that had emerged from the sessions. After completing a number of these workshops Van Tyne compiled his major suggestions and published them in the popular NSL pamphlet, *Democracy's Education Problem.*[40] In addition to his traditional plea to forget the old "redcoat" image of the British and establish stronger Anglo-American ties, he urged teachers to point out the contrasts between American democracy and German autocracy. Instead of just presenting students "mere dry facts" about comparative governmental systems, teachers should show American freedom of action as opposed to German "blind obedience of orders to do cruel and brutal acts." The contrasts in national types could also be brought down to an individual level. "Would it not be instructive to put side by side in our readers quotations revealing the ideals of the typical Prussian, Frederick the Great, and the typical American, George Washington, or of the German hero, Bismarck, and of the American hero, Abraham Lincoln?" This technique of comparative quotations had worked well for the NSL on speaker's platforms and in pamphlets, so Van Tyne saw no reason why it would not be equally effective in the classroom.

Considering the diversity of the NSL summer schools, coordinators, teachers, and sessions, it is safe to assume that repercussions were commensurately diverse. As was customary with much of the League's war work, the execution of this campaign depended upon individuals and unfortunately the few records they kept concentrate on planning and publicity rather than implementation. Judging from the number of teachers who participated and the amounts of time, energy, and printed material expended, the NSL philosophy of "100 per cent Americanism" probably filtered into an increasingly large number of classrooms. The many enthusiastic letters that McElroy and Van Tyne received from teachers and school administrators testified to the popularity of their message. Amor-

40 For further discussion of the pamphlet, see chapter 3 above.

phous and xenophobic as it was, the League program found a large and eager clientele willing to transmit its ideas to young captive audiences.

The last major propaganda project aimed at classrooms came from the CPI and presented several paradoxes. The *National School Service*, a tabloid newspaper for schoolteachers, achieved more success than the majority of propaganda attempts in accomplishing its stated goals, yet it began to circulate only two months before the armistice. The CPI's two regular historians, Ford and Harding, closely supervised its publication despite the fact that the paper contained little that required the services of trained hisorians. At its inception the editors had not even planned to use the paper as propaganda until results proved that elementary schools provided one of the most fertile areas for cultivating patriotism.

The *National School Service* emerged as a byproduct of the myriad agencies that flourished during the war. Because so many federal and private officials tried to enlist participation from schoolchildren, they overwhelmed teachers with appeals for support. To correct this situation the CPI decided to publish a newspaper to be sent free to 600,000 public school teachers. Supplementing its regular educational features would be space for organizations such as Red Cross, Food Administration, War Stamps, Loyalty Loans, and others wishing to carry their crusades into classrooms and homes. By coordinating all the material into one biweekly, sixteen-page paper the CPI hoped to lighten the teachers' burden and make the solicitations more effective. The paper also gave the federal govrnment its first opportunity to reach the schools simultaneously with news, suggestions, and regulations.[41]

Ford explained in the first issue that neither the government nor the editors of the paper wanted the American teacher to become an "intellectual drill sergeant of national prejudices." Instead he indicated that this new medium of suggestion and coordination offered the educator a chance to render greater national service by making the war more vital to students. The emphasis would be pragmatic rather than philosophical, he added, and the paper would

[41] G. S. Ford, "America's Fight for Public Opinion," *Minnesota History Bulletin* 3 (February 1919), p. 25.

concentrate on material for elementary students.[42] Even though Ford supervised the overall production of the paper and Harding edited the historical material using his experience in children's literature, neither was one of the actual editors. This task fell to William C. Bagley, a professor of education at Columbia and former colleague of Ford's at Illinois, and to James Searson, an English professor doing graduate work at Columbia during the war. Lacking a formal title, Ford still remained the dominant force and his personal touch permeated all aspects of the publication. His keynote message in the first issue shared space with welcoming salutations from George Creel and President Wilson, all written by Ford. He later admitted that this double chore of ghost writing placed a real strain on his powers of stylistic variation, and it indicates the ubiquitous nature of his influence on the paper.[43]

Within its sixteen pages the paper offered a kaleidoscopic array of news, songs, patriotic games, poetry, and tips for children to help in the war effort. Quotable quatrains such as

> Hush little Thrift stamp,
> Don't you cry;
> You'll be a War Bond
> By and by,

and arithmetic problems which asked "if John saves five cents each day for five days, how many Thrift Stamps can he buy?" made the economics of war a personal concern of young students.[44] Simplistic stories for explaining the war managed to incorporate lessons in elementary diplomacy as well as a vicarious participation in the war:

> Do any of you know anyone who has gone away to be a soldier? Where did he go? Why has he gone? Why are we fighting the Germans? What did they do to our ships? Suppose a German airplane should fly over our city. What would happen to us?

[42] *National School Service*, 1 September 1918, pp. 8-9.
[43] G. S. Ford, "Reminiscences," Columbia Oral History Collection, copy at University of Minnesota Library, 2: 376-77.
[44] *National School Service*, 1 October 1918, p. 13.

That is why father or brother has gone—to show them that they must not sink our ships, to drive them out of the countries where they have been burning and killing.[45]

The paper also used atrocity material with greater sophistication and emotional impact than the CPI had formerly employed. To illustrate a feature story on German use of poison gas, the editors printed photographs of small European children and animals all fitted out with special gasmasks to protect them from German "frightfulness."[46] The austerity crusades which accompanied lessons on the necessity for voluntary rationing further exemplify the method of persuasion. After telling of the soldiers' need for more boots and leather goods, the *National School Service* taught children how to protect their footwear—"Do not slide; do not scuff your feet"—and offered for memorization such aphorisms as "waste is treason. To save is to serve."[47]

The manner of presenting this information was as unaffected and straightforward as the young audiences for which it was intended. Part of the paper's success came from this casual approach and the lack of academic self-consciousness which the editors displayed. Creel later called the *National School Service* the CPI's "most unique and effective publication."[48] The paper succeeded admirably in its dual aims of coordinating recruitment material and making the war an integral part of the school day. The popularity of the paper, particularly in rural areas, was so great that President Wilson transferred it to the Department of the Interior after the war instead of immediately discontinuing its publication, as planned. Credit for this success should go to propagandists who happened to be historians, not the reverse. Ford, Harding, and their assistants temporarily discarded their historical training and used other talents to translate the war into the language of children.

The propaganda work done by historians for educational purposes presents a curious irony. These historians were educators

45 Ibid., 1 September 1918, p. 12.
46 Ibid., 15 October 1918, pp. 1, 2.
47 Ibid., 1 September 1918, p. 13; 15 October 1918, p. 8.
48 George Creel, *How We Advertised America* (New York, 1920), p. 111.

by vocation, but when they elected to play the part of propagandists during the war they hesitated to perform their new role in their accustomed arena, the classroom. Whether this was because they anticipated a short war in which there would be little need to mobilize or indoctrinate the younger generation, or because they preferred the temporary freedom of nonacademic activity to the professional restrictions of formal education, their initial work in the schools was scattered and unenthusiastic. As the war progressed and their offerings to educators increased, the historians' ambivalence became apparent, noticeably in the NBHS articles for the *History Teacher's Magazine* and the ill-fated war issues course. By the end of the war their programs of patriotic instruction were more comprehensive, more successful as propaganda, and only tangentially related to their profession. Ironically, and not illogically, their most effective propaganda in the classroom employed their talents as educators rather than as historians. If historians had turned to the classroom sooner and if their educational programs had shown more orchestration and less improvisation, schools might have proved a better medium for patriotic service than they did.

VII. Criticisms & Conclusions

When the armistice came in early November 1918, Americans began demobilizing their war mechanism as enthusiastically as they had thrown it together a year and a half before. Military, industrial, and humanitarian agencies evacuated Washington and emergency programs disappeared like the last scrawny turnips uprooted from victory gardens only a few weeks earlier. The cheers that greeted returning soldiers served hopefully as final applause for a drama reluctantly staged and now thankfully over. Although the guns were now silent and the physical machinery of war dismantled, Americans found that much of the war effort, particularly the intellectual mobilization, would not dissolve into memory as swiftly as they might hope. The diplomats at Versailles and the historian-propagandists encountered continuing reminders of their wartime activities, often magnified and distorted beyond reality. The Versailles negotiators faced the Bourbons' ornate hall of mirrors and could escape the reflections in time; historians confronted less opaque reminders in the form of critical reassessments that lingered long after the other images of war had faded.

One of the liveliest indications that the historians' propaganda work would not die unchallenged appeared in 1920 in an article by America's foremost iconoclast, Henry L. Mencken. With a position somewhere between contempt and comedy Mencken labeled the professors "Star Spangled Men" and advocated establishing a Distinguished Service Order to commemorate their actions. He singled out NSL and CPI historians and listed their slavish support of Wilson's war policies, their suppression of the German language and questionable literature, and the controversial Sisson documents as odious manifestations of their perfervid patriotism. As a prize for the most accomplished of the propagandists he proposed to enliven their academic garb with "the grand cross of the order . . . a gold badge in polychrome enamel and stained glass, a baldric of the national colors, a violet plug hat with a sunburst on the side," and an annual pension to compensate them for prostituting their professional ethics.[1] Not to be taken with complete seriousness, Mencken's attack nonetheless publicized the fact that a few Americans were unhappy with the wartime behavior of their professors and were not content to let the episode go without public reprimand.

Earlier and less public reprimands for the historians came as much from the political associations of the committees in which they worked as from reactions against their professional conduct. Both the CPI and the NSL made bitter enemies during the war for reasons separate from academic ethics, and because the historians were among the most public representatives of these two groups, they received much of the criticism. As scholars they had been accustomed to the relative decorum of campus life; now as public figures engaged in manipulation of mass opinion, they worked with unfamiliar political and literary personalities in an atmosphere charged with patriotism, hate, and hysteria. Frequently the company they kept used this frenetic situation for personal advancement and the resulting partisan crossfire involved the historians, often against their wishes and usually to their detriment.

Ford and the CPI historians felt the sting of political criticism the soonest of the three groups, probably because their official attachment to the government made them more vulnerable to attack from antiadministration forces. Many Republicans in Congress had never fully recognized Wilson as the nation's legitimate spokesman because both of his presidential elections had brought him only precarious victory margins. When he appointed George Creel director of the CPI, conservative Republicans increased their opposition, for Creel's espousal of radical progressive measures was well known. No matter how critical the president's opponents might be of his war program they had to maintain a certain discretion in their public statements lest they be branded unpatriotic, even traitors. But if politics were set aside on higher levels, the CPI offered an exposed lower flank of the administration that critics could attack without damaging their reputations. Creel was

[1] Henry L. Mencken, "Star Spangled Men," *New Republic* 24 (29 September 1920: 119.

a large target, due in part to his intimate contact with war agencies and also because he cultivated the image of being "the other self of the President."[2]

The irony of much of the Republican criticism is that it was intended for Wilson, aimed at Creel, and hit the historians. Representative James F. Byrnes of South Carolina, a Democratic supporter of Wilson, pointed out that the critics were using Creel and the CPI as a "goat" in lieu of other avenues for getting their opinions on record,[3] and they found it easier to attack the CPI pamphlets than any other aspect of the organization because they were plentiful and permanent. Senator Porter P. McCumber of North Dakota mentioned no names when he deplored the tons of Marxist literature being circulated around the country by the CPI, but Senator Harry New of Indiana told an Indianapolis audience the authors were "Mr. Creel, with his bunch of Socialistic, muck-raking misfits."[4] Besides having his historians branded socialists, Ford, who was a Republican, had to withstand constant abuse of his scholars' prose style, again aimed incorrectly at Creel. Senator Lawrence Sherman of Illinois said the writing was "aimed at shock rather than sense" and that its "brilliancy is the glow of putrescence, it shines with the fitful glimmer of decay."[5] Ideologically and stylistically Republican critics maligned the CPI historians while probably not being aware of the actual authors of the pamphlets.

Politically motivated and frequently irrational, this criticism nevertheless had an unsettling effect on the historians. J. Franklin Jameson told one congressman that the CPI historians were unselfish, upright, efficient, intelligent, and undeserving of the carping political abuse that landed in their laps despite their not being the original targets. He felt the partisan attacks on Creel and the CPI "have tended to obscure the real merits of the work."[6] Some historians feared that their reputations might be damaged if in-

[2] *New York Times*, 14 May 1918, p. 10.
[3] U. S., *Congressional Record*, 65 Cong., 2 sess., p. 7914.
[4] Ibid., p. 7289; *New York Times*, 30 May 1918, p. 11.
[5] U. S., *Congressional Record*, 65 Cong., 2 sess., p. 8990.
[6] Jameson to Representative Frederick H. Gillett (copy), 27 June 1918, Box 28, File 391, Jameson Papers, Manuscript Division, Library of Congress.

volved in these controversies. Ford's unsuccessful attempts to get Notestein to accept a full-time CPI position exemplified this situation. Notestein had remained aloof, preferring to do his work away from Washington or through the NBHS because "the Creel Bureau seems a bad thing to tie up to. I know something of Ford's difficulties with it, though he has never said a word."[7] The little that Ford did say about his problems in the CPI either smoothed over the difficulties with innocuous comments or displayed a resignation to the occupational hazards of being a political employee. He admitted that the criticism was severe and largely engendered by Creel, but that without Creel, the CPI "would have early made its appearance in the obituary column," thus leaving historians with fewer opportunities for war service.[8]

Unlike the CPI, the NSL's involvement in politics came from choice rather than indirection and sustained even more public criticism. The League had been one of the most outspoken advocates of military preparedness since 1915, and as early as May 1918 had begun to push for a postwar program of universal military training. Some questions arose concerning the motives for this continued militancy and the League's role in the congressional elections of 1918 intensified these questions. While Wilson asked voters to send back to Washington a Democratic majority, the NSL asked for a rejection of all members of the Sixty-fifth Congress who had shown a lack of patriotism by voting "wrong" on specific war measures. It circulated a list of legislators who it felt had deviated from NSL-favored programs, and campaigned against them in primaries and the November general elections. A closer examination of the list revealed that the "acid test" of loyalty favored partisan Republicanism and opposition to government restrictions on corporations as much as it favored active support of the war.[9] Other than helping to defeat a few socialist candidates the NSL

[7] Notestein to E. B. Greene, 12 May 1918, Box 12, NBHS Records.

[8] U. S., Congress, House, *Sundry Civil Bill, 1919: Hearings before Subcommittee of House Committee on Appropriations*, part 3, *Committee on Public Information*, 65 Cong., 2 sess. (Washington, D. C., 1918), p. 163.

[9] NSL form letter, 24 July 1918, NSL Folder, Albert Shaw Papers, New York Public Library; Robert D. Ward, "The Origin and Activities of the National Security League, 1914-1919," *MVHR* 47 (June 1960): 61-62.

campaign exerted minimal influence on the election; it did prompt
an angry outburst from congressmen who felt their loyalty im-
pugned and it resulted in a rancorous investigation of the NSL.

The congressional hearings, which lasted from December 1918
through February 1919, dispelled all doubts about NSL partisanship and opened fresh attacks on its historian-propagandists.
Chaired by Kentucky's Ben Johnson, this lame-duck Democratic
committee set out to investigate the League's activity in the elections, and, after testimony from congressmen and League officials,
decided that the organization, with its financial and political
practices, had violated the Corrupt Practices Act of 1910.[10] No
legal action came from these findings but public reaction did sour
on the NSL when supplementary testimony revealed their complicity with possible war profiteers. The committee auditors found
that a large portion of League funds came from powerful industrial
and financial sources such as Henry C. Frick, Cornelius Vanderbilt,
John D. Rockefeller, and the Carnegie Corporation, which stood
to gain, consciously or not, from continued military spending.[11]
This presented a picture considerably less attractive than the one
of thousands of patriotic citizens whom the NSL had credited with
small contributions. In light of these embarrassing revelations and
increasingly hostile questions, Robert McElroy proved a poor
witness for scholars working with the NSL. His brief appearance
before the committee was sullen and intransigent and gave unwitting credence to the characterization by Wisconsin's Edward
E. Brown that McElroy was "absolutely unfit, and of such a
poverty of judgement that he ought not to go out under the
auspices of any society and be their spokesman."[12]

McElroy treated the committee report with the same contempt
he had shown its congressional authors. In a three-page refutation
published shortly after the hearings adjourned, he charged that
the investigation had "failed to disclose anything inconsistent
with the high ideals of disinterested patriotic service professed by

[10] U. S., Congress, House, *Investigation of National Security League*, report no.
1173, 3 March 1919, 65 Cong., 3 sess. (Washington, D. C., 1919). This brief
report accompanied the multi-volume NSL *Hearings*.

[11] Ward, "NSL," pp. 54, 64.

[12] *NSL Hearings*, 11: 933.

the League." He complained, moreover, that the committee had concentrated on politics and had ignored the major work of the League, that of the speaking, writing, and education work under his direction.[13] McElroy had somehow overlooked the testimony involving the education work of his close NSL associate, Van Tyne. Representative Brown read into the record some of Van Tyne's writing concerning the professor's desire to deemphasize Anglo-American antagonisms by restructuring the teaching of the American Revolution. Obviously a Whig at heart and in disagreement with this revised approach, Brown said that Van Tyne was not a "safe man to go around through the country and educate the youth of the country."[14] Most of these exchanges were just so much political rhetoric, but no matter how poorly grounded they received a public airing and served to arouse distrust for historians who kept the company of alleged war profiteers and political opportunists. This guilt-by-association tended to discredit in a collective fashion those historians who had participated in propaganda.

Historians wounded tangentially by political opponents became targets for even more direct abuse as the disparate critics of the war began to coalesce in the ranks of revisionism during the decade after the armistice. As the most articulate spokesmen of the war effort—and in the case of the CPI historians, the official voice of it—they were susceptible to much of the criticism leveled at the administration policies concerning war causation and American involvement. Even before the war ended the crippled and bitter pacifist of Greenwich Village, Randolph Bourne, had pointed out that "there is work to be done to prevent this war of ours from passing into popular mythology as a holy crusade."[15] This invitation to rebuke Wilsonian idealism became the keynote of many American historians during the 1920s and 1930s and revisionism

---

13 McElroy, "Statement on Behalf of the National Security League upon the Report of the Special Committee of the House of Representatives . . ." (New York, 1919), n.p.

14 *NSL Hearings*, 6: 515.

15 Bourne, "War and the Intellectuals," *Seven Arts* (June 1917), reprinted in *Untimely Papers* (New York, 1919), p. 45.

grew into an academic and publishing industry in itself, bringing notoriety to such authors as Harry Elmer Barnes, C. Hartley Grattan, Walter Millis, and others who questioned official positions on war issues. The primary consideration here is not the respective arguments of these men but an analysis of the events which brought on the wave of reappraisals and the effect they had on the historian-propagandists who had helped to popularize the positions now under attack.

The obvious impropriety of Section 231 of the Versailles Treaty —the famous German war guilt clause—was that the peace conference had revealed that Germany had not been exclusively responsible for the four years of bloodshed. The lengthy peace discussions brought to light the tangled series of secret alliances, national prejudices, and mercenary motives for expansion of many of the belligerents, making the inclusion of Secion 231 a self-serving gesture by the victorious powers. The rapid accessibility of published correspondence, memoirs, and official diplomatic and military documents also testified to the fact that no one could clearly allot guilt or innocence to any nation. This overlapping of wartime charges with postwar reappraisals created embarrassment for statesmen and historians alike. Coming as it did so soon after the armistice this divided stance intensified the questioning mood and growing disenchantment that prevailed in America. The final Senate rejection of the Versailles Treaty and the presidential election of 1920 seemed to indicate a repudiation of the things that Wilson and his disciples had stood for, including the intellectual buttresses of America's war effort.

The first scholarly manifestation of this new look at war causation appeared in the *American Historical Review* in 1920 and compounded the irony of the shifting positions. J. Franklin Jameson had commissioned a three-part series by Sidney B. Fay to review some of the new information available on the war. The articles came to be known as the New Light series. They exposed as myths the stories of German plots to foment war and revealed that tensions between other nations helped bring on the conflict. Fay's scholarship did not absolve Germany of all responsibility, but it did reduce its criminal status by extending the guilt to

Austria and indirectly to Russia and to poor communications and bumbling by the other powers.[16] This collaboration of Jameson and Fay was in part a tacit about-face for the *Review* and the two principals. Jameson had used the pages of the journal during the war to herald and publicize the work of the NBHS and Fay had contributed material to the CPI's *War Cyclopedia*. Both organizations had given credence to the sole-guilt theory and had used professional historians to grant respectability to the arguments. Now in 1920 two of the participants, in a reversal of positions, created a paradigm for the new approaches to war historiography, the most famous of which was that of Harry Elmer Barnes.

According to Barnes, Fay's New Light articles were the catalyst which prompted him to revise the attitudes perpetuated by wartime propaganda. His disenchantment with his own propaganda work for the NSL and other agencies was already beginning to surface in 1920 while he taught at Clark University. When he read the first article in the *Review* his disillusion with his former position crystallized into a desire to rectify it. He said that the new look at war causation undermined his long devotion to Shotwell and other wartime propagandists in a fashion similar to his youthful discovery that Santa Claus was a myth.[17] Whether his revisionism was an attempt to seek intellectual absolution for his propaganda sins or a sincere desire to restructure what he felt were historical inaccuracies, Barnes waged a crusade of unmatched tenacity that lasted until his death in 1968. His affair with the facts of history is a matter of public record; his controversies with the historian-propagandists are less well known and of more immediate interest.

Barnes began his crusade with a series of minor articles and book reviews during the early 1920s, but his first systematic attacks began in 1924 when he reviewed Charles D. Hazen's revised textbook, *Europe since 1815*. The *New Republic*'s editor, Herbert Croly, had long been critical of Wilson's administration and urged Barnes to display his historical integrity by exposing the Wilsonian

---

16 Fay, "New Light on the Origins of the World War," AHR 25 (July 1920): 616-39; 26 (October 1920): 37-53; 26 (January 1921): 225-54.

17 Barnes to author, 13 April 1968; Warren Cohen, *The American Revisionists: The Lessons of Intervention in World War I* (Chicago, 1967), p. 36.

bias found in the treatment of events surrounding the war.[18] With this first major jump into the revisionist debate Barnes must have taken delight in the fact that Hazen had been an active pamphleteer for the CPI; Barnes had been involved in an ugly fracas with the CPI during the war and this opportunity could act as partial retribution for what he considered a past injustice. He had not forgotten the CPI's criticism of his own pamphleteering work for the NSL and the intimation that he was not "painstaking and honest in historical investigation."[19] In his dissection of Hazen's book Barnes turned this intimation back on Hazen and the CPI collectively, pointing out that the mobilized historians "behaved like clerks or shopmen in the capitulation to herd pressures and hysteria." Specifically he accused Hazen of having failed to discard his propagandist's mantle when returning to the world of scholarship. Barnes found Hazen's theory of German war guilt "grotesquely misleading" and charged that the "1917 stories of German frightfulness and submarine atrocities are repeated in full and without the slightest qualification."[20] Subsequent issues of the *New Republic* became a battleground which drew in other historians and issues, proving little except that Barnes had become an agitator of no mean accomplishment.

Current History Magazine accelerated this growing academic debate by compiling a forum of historians' opinions on the traditional war theories and Barnes's new scale of war guilt, beginning with Austria and running with declining responsibility through Russia, France, Germany, and Britain. A. B. Hart led the attack on his former NSL associate in an emotional dissent from the revisionist's new evidence and interpretation: "The subject is too involved, the underlying race and language antipathies are too strong, the confusion of relations in Eastern Europe too complex to make any review of printed testimony a safe basis for changing an opinion which was forged by the fires of war."[21] *The Nation*

[18] William Neumann, "Harry Elmer Barnes as World War I Revisionist," in Arthur Goddard, ed., *Harry Elmer Barnes: Learned Crusader* (Colorado Springs, 1968), p. 265.

[19] Barnes to G. S. Ford, 17 July 1917, Box 1, NBHS Records.

[20] Barnes, book review in *New Republic* 38 (19 March 1924): 10-14.

[21] Hart, *Current History Magazine* 20 (May 1924): 196.

jumped quickly and uninvited into the forum, asking what right a historian had to "permit any opinion to be forged by the fires, the passion, the bitterness, the hatreds of the War," and clucked its disapproval of Hart's continuing adherence to his NSL positions of six years' vintage.[22] Most of the other historians in the forum, such as Bernadotte Schmitt, Frank M. Anderson, and Charles Seymour, would not go as far as Hart in rejecting revisionism, and neither would they accept all of Barnes's theories. Carl L. Becker, however, could find no reason to disagree with the new approach, revealing the distance he had traveled from the CPI-NBHS. He predicted that the Barnes material under debate would be "widely acclaimed in this country."[23]

Lionized by the swelling legions of the disenchanted, Barnes intensified his crusade by publishing in 1926 his own full-length treatment, *The Genesis of the World War*. Therein he decried those who had touted the war as noble, just, and holy, and hoped that the work of the revisionists would help to combat the "propaganda of those who will announce the necessity and idealism of the next war."[24] The book engendered a predictable number of debates among historians and Barnes compiled these exchanges in 1928 in a volume entitled *In Quest of Truth and Justice*. This anthology of articles, reviews, and letters revealed the emotionalism and polarization of views that characterized the debate over revisionism. Among those singled out for abuse was William Stearns Davis, whom Barnes lambasted for his CPI pamphleteering and his other literary "fairy tales." Also taken to task was Earl E. Sperry, with whom Barnes had done anonymous work in publishing the NSL pamphlet *Tentacles of the German Octopus*. Barnes forgave himself and Sperry for having done the work during the heat of the war, but condemned his collaborator for still believing the work valid.[25]

Barnes's accusations were both public and personal, and his opponents, or victims as it were, remained for the most part

22 118 (21 May 1924): 576.
23 *Current History Magazine* 20 (June 1924): 456.
24 Harry Elmer Barnes, *The Genesis of the World War: An Introduction to the Problems of War Guilt* (New York, 1926), pp. xi-xii.
25 Idem, *In Quest of Truth and Justice* (Chicago, 1928), pp. 227, 277.

silent. He later recalled that "I was not attacked very much . . . although there was plenty of sub-rosa abuse and hostility."[26] Perhaps the historians chose not to dignify his more intemperate charges by engaging in public personality assassinations, or perhaps they decided to dismiss their war work as avocational pursuits which needed neither fanfare nor defense. Barnes chose to believe the latter, saying that the propagandists preferred to let the matter ride "rather than revive knowledge of what they had said and supported during the war."[27] Even if this was not the case, he was correct in his assessment of the amount of "sub-rosa abuse" circulating among his opponents. William Stearns Davis delighted in telling a friend that he had found several people "that dislike Harry Elmer Barnes more than I do (which is saying something)," among them being A. B. Hart.[28] Jameson consoled one of Barnes's more severely wounded victims, Bernadotte Schmitt, that "never in my rather long lifetime, I am sure, has any American professor ever gone so far in insolence, or for that matter, in the exhibition of self-conceit. . . . it ought to kill him, so far as any standing in our profession is concerned."[29]

If Barnes's demise was not forthcoming his standing in the profession remained controversial and many historians regarded him as a pariah. He continued to lash out at both the men and the ideas that had been a part of Wilson's idealistic war. In his textbook of historical writing published in 1937 he mixed with his discussions of Herodotus and Hegel a disapproving sermon on the war historians who broke from their intellectual moorings and cheapened the historical profession. As late as 1962, when his text was revised, he still devoted four pages to the indiscretions of the CPI and NBHS and listed for infamy the names of Shotwell, Ford, Hazen, Schmitt, and Davis, and then added his NSL collab-

---

26 Barnes to author, 13 April 1968.
27 Ibid.
28 Davis to August C. Krey, 5 July 1926, Folder 197, Krey Papers, University of Minnesota Library.
29 J. F. Jameson to Schmitt, 14 January 1927 (copy), Box 80, File 1497, Jameson Papers. Barnes had earlier assumed Schmitt to a revisionist ally and then attacked him with particular severity when Schmitt turned out to be less of a revisionist than was anticipated.

orators, Hart, McElroy, Sperry, Thayer, and Van Tyne.[30] Silent as they may have been in the face of his attacks, the historians could take solace in what amounted to his professional ostracism. The historical organizations and journals disapproved of and disregarded him except as a point of reference, and his career developed along the outer edges of the historical craft in sociology, economics, and philosophy. Many of the mobilized historians went so far as to consider abuse from Barnes a badge of merit on the assumption that his criticism heightened their respectability. One of these was Wallace Notestein, who escaped Barnes's attacks but recalled that he would have felt honored to have been a member of the maligned group.[31] Many other historians lamented his personal style and sledgehammer approach while adopting his academic conclusions, and revisionism—minus the name-calling—became a widely accepted school of historical writing. By the time Charles C. Tansill's *America Goes to War* appeared in 1938, revisionism had become more scholarly, temperate, and respectable while still tracing its lineage back to the heated exposures by Barnes.

One direct disciple of Barnes who slammed the historians with perhaps the most severe broadside of all was C. Hartley Grattan. Too young to have been involved in the war, he entered Clark University in 1920 and fell under the spell of Barnes when the latter was just beginning his revisionist crusade. Grattan's career lies mainly in the realm of literary criticism and international journalism but he took every Barnes history course he could while at Clark and learned much about the revisionist debate in private conversation with his professor. Barnes introduced Grattan to H. L. Mencken, then editing the *American Mercury*, and from this new friendship came one of the most pointed attacks on the scholars' war activity. Grattan admitted that he "was in ardent search of reputation (or was it notoriety?)" and his commissions from Mencken guided him in that direction.[32] Until his book

[30] Harry Elmer Barnes, A *History of Historical Writing*, 2d rev. ed. (New York, 1962), pp. 279-80.
[31] Notestein to author, 27 August 1967.
[32] Grattan to author, 16 April 1968.

Why We Fought appeared in 1929, his greatest gift to the movement was a bravura performance of selective research, "The
Historians Cut Loose," which the *American Mercury* printed in
its August 1927 issue. Designed to discredit the wartime historians and their theories, the exposé allowed no quarter; the
men who fronted for the state were "to be incinerated" for their
actions.[33] Grattan drew no distinctions between the CPI, the NBHS,
and the NSL, finding all the historians equally guilty of falling
into the debauch of patriotic service and issuing "official bun-
combe" that would make Clio blush.[34]

The article was actually a joint product of Grattan, Barnes,
and Mencken. Grattan culled the wartime publications of the
three organizations and the individual historians to find embarrassing passages of anti-Germanism or excessive patriotism. This
would not have been difficult in 1918; it was easier in 1927 since
nine years and much cynicism had replaced the war effusions.
After selecting the quotations and constructing a draft of the
presentation he turned over the manuscript to Mencken and
Barnes, who "collaborated on the rather acerb frosting of the
poisoned cake."[35] The result was an anthology of damning testimony from the mouths of the historian-propagandists strung together with equally damaging personality sketches. As a kind of
poetic injustice, this technique closely resembled the CPI-NSL
pamphlets that had used the same method on German figures.
The article credited William Roscoe Thayer with the "most
astonishing nonsense of all," and allowed him to quote again his
famous League "moral eunuch" speech. A. B. Hart took honors
as "one of the most violent of the warlocks" whose *America at War*
handbook for speakers was guilty of distorting such Mencken
favorites as Nietzsche and Treitschke. Robert McElroy emerged
as indiscrete and intolerant but a "star performer" for the NSL,
and the article ran through his unfortunate paces at the University
of Wisconsin Stock Pavilion once more. Grattan caught Claude
Van Tyne red-handed perverting history textbooks, found Earl

[33] Ibid.
[34] Grattan, "Historians Cut Loose," p. 422.
[35] Grattan to author, 16 April 1968.

Sperry guilty of xenophobia, and labeled William Stearns Davis a sensationalist and a gossip.[36]

As in the case of Barnes's criticism, Grattan received few public rebuttals from the historians he had attacked. Perhaps the scholars had become accustomed to such charges from revisionists or perhaps, as Grattan assessed the silence, "it was a case of the less said the better."[37] For whatever reason silence prevailed. When Grattan's full-length treatment of American entry in the war appeared in 1929, the revisionists publicized it as a boon to their cause, and conversely, no major professional journal reviewed it; hence it did not gain official recognition at the time as a scholarly contribution to the field. Grattan had quoted on his title page Bourne's plea to prevent the war from becoming mythologized into a noble crusade, and, if nothing else, Grattan had helped to accomplish this.

Few scholars were still quoting Wilson's pristine phrases in 1929 to explain the war; likewise few had become total revisionists in their scholarship. The work of Grattan, Barnes, and others helped to accelerate the pace of rhetorical disengagement from the wartime mentality and compelled the historian-propagandists to look more closely at their recent activities in service to the state. The abrasiveness and emotionalism of their approach often blunted or negated their intentions and sometimes drove the old-line historians such as Hart into a harder defense of their positions. They did manage to draw into the public eye in popular books and periodicals scholars who had once been known or discussed only in academic circles, and they forced historians to recognize that public service made them subject to public criticism and that their positions were as vulnerable as were those of the politicians they served. The revisionists created temporary embarrassment and personality clashes, and effected a more searching analysis of the diplomacy of war, but their impact on the subsequent lives and careers of the embattled historians was slight to the point of being negligible.

---

[36] Grattan, "Historians Cut Loose," passim.
[37] Grattan to author, 16 April 1968.

Neither the propaganda work nor the attacks on it seem to have affected the careers of the participants. For the most part they regarded their extraordinary venture into patriotic service as an aberrant chapter in their lives, an atypical departure from scholarship necessitated by the national crisis and obviating judgment by professional standards. Their lives and careers would return to normal with the armistice in the same way as military, scientific, and medical participants in the war effort would resume prewar activities, overcoming the brief but troublesome disruption caused by the international conflict. Of the dozen or so historians who did major and conspicuous propaganda work—work which the public could easily link with their names—none were adversely affected in their careers nor were their reputations besmirched. Most resumed, maintained, and enhanced their status within the profession, some even becoming exemplars in the craft. This uninterrupted progress in their careers came neither because of nor despite their work as propagandists; it came as a matter of scholarly achievement. Time and the academic world apparently agreed with the propagandists that the war work was aberrant and not to be appended to their credentials. Beneath the public amnesia regarding their controversial work, the private assessments that the historians gave their war effort were usually brief, and with few exceptions, ingratiating. Autobiographical historians are few, thus hindering the search for their personal reactions. Beyond the few who left formal memoirs, one must piece together their self-appraisals from fugitive correspondence, random comments, oblique references in their later writing, and indirectly from the things they chose to omit when discussing their careers.

The case of Guy Stanton Ford is perhaps the easiest to handle. He spoke and wrote frequently of his work in the CPI and the same reaction appears with metronomic regularity. Between the time when he wrote the chapter draft on the CPI historians for Creel's *How We Advertised America* in 1920, and 1954-1955 when he recorded his oral memoirs, his expressed opinion remained static: "I left the committee at the end of the war with the feeling that I would never regret or renege on anything that I did then. I never have, and have never had a real occasion to do so.

In making major decisions I had not been swayed by the passions of the moment, or gone off the deep end about it."[38] He readily admitted that "probably all of the publications of the Creel Committee have some defect,"[39] but just as readily submitted the autobiographical material to *Who's Who in America* that he and his historians had helped to produce the 75,000,000 pieces of CPI literature, no matter if flawed. He did advise University of Minnesota students early in 1940 that the CPI type of propaganda was now outdated, that present attempts would have to be more subtle, and that the "old horror and atrocity stories won't do any more."[40] This shift of emphasis chronicles a change in times rather than intention. When America entered war again in 1941, Ford answered the call once more by helping the War Department to edit educational pamphlets for army discussion groups, and he eagerly described this work in the *American Historical Review*.[41] Ford's place in the profession reinforced his consistent belief in the acceptability of patriotic service; a career that was already respected and secure took on added luster, unaffected by what critics said about "court historians." In addition to his continued writing and his teaching and administrative duties at Minnesota, he served on the executive committee of the Mississippi Valley Historical Association from 1920 to 1923 and on the board of editors of the *American Historical Review* from 1921 to 1927. His colleagues awarded him the presidency of the American Historical Association in 1937, and from 1941 to 1953 he edited the *American Historical Review*, positions not generally held by apostates.

A. B. Hart's postwar statements displayed a spirited defense of his war work and an irascible contempt for its critics. Shortly after the war he testified before a Senate subcommittee on the topic of German propaganda and his position seemed to have grown even more aggressive than it had been during the war. He

---

[38] Chapter manuscript for *How We Advertised America*, with notations, Folder 163, Ford Papers, University of Minnesota Library; Ford, "Reminiscences," Columbia Oral History Collection, copy at University of Minnesota Library, 2: 419.

[39] Ford, "Reminiscences," 2: 394.

[40] *Minnesota Daily*, 27 January 1940, clipping in Folder 163, Ford Papers.

[41] 50 (April 1945): 644.

reviewed some of the publications that he had written, including the NSL pamphlets and handbooks, and pointed out that if they could have been more patriotic or helpful to the Allied cause he was unaware of how because they were extensions of his personality and he was "a consistent permanent anti-German."[42] Following the hearing he continued to assail the enemy who had "set out to overcome the United States by a campaign of darkness and who left a serpent's trail of hatred and falsehood," indicating that the cessation of hostilities had not altered his national views.[43] When the revisionist debate began to rage in 1924 Hart regarded it as an attack on all that he had worked for and still believed in. He charged that if the revisionists were right then "Roosevelt was wrong, Wilson was wrong, Elihu Root was wrong, Ambassador Page was wrong, everybody was wrong," a position which he had no intention of accepting, at least in public.[44] At age seventy with almost every scholarly honor already in his possession and dozens of books to his credit, Hart could well afford to dismiss as inconsequential such brief unpleasantries as war propaganda; he was virtually unassailable. Even after retiring from his teaching career he continued to write and edit from his office atop Harvard's Widener Library, becoming a public authority on George Washington as he directed the nation's bicentennial celebration of the first president's birth. When he died in 1943, approaching ninety, most of his contemporaries were willing to accept his "fallibilities and explosions" as mere colorful adornments to the career of "the most useful historical worker of his generation."[45]

The war had a curious impact on the lives and careers of Claude H. Van Tyne and Andrew C. McLaughlin; it almost destroyed the close personal relationship enjoyed by the two men while leaving their professional reputations untarnished. Van Tyne resembled

---

[42] U. S., Congress, Senate, *Brewing and Liquor Interests and German Propaganda: Hearings before a Subcommittee on the Judiciary*, 65 Cong., 2 and 3 sess. (Washington, D. C., 1919), 2: 1626, 1633.

[43] Hart, "The Trail of the German: From the Reminiscences of Albert Bushnell Hart," typed manuscript, 20 December 1918, p. 4, Hart Papers, New York Public Library.

[44] Hart, "A Dissent from the Conclusions of Professor Barnes," *Current History Magazine* 20 (May 1924): 195-96.

[45] *New York Times*, 18 June 1943, p. 20; *AHR* 49 (October 1943): 192-94.

Hart in that his defense of NSL issues stiffened after the war. This continuing hard-line approach to American involvement in the war indicated that his militant stance with League programs was more than just a temporary wave of patriotism, thus precluding any embarrassed second thoughts about his propaganda work of 1917-1918. His changing relations with the considerably more restrained McLaughlin illustrated this situation. The two had taught together at Michigan and had collaborated in 1911 in publishing a textbook, *History of the United States for Schools,* but saw their partnership strain as the war developed. Even before American entry their positions had begun to diverge sharply, Van Tyne publicly urging an aggressive response to German provocations and McLaughlin privately lecturing him about extremist positions that departed from "decency, honesty, and common sense."[46] The NSL and the NBHS likewise parted company in their approach to propaganda and Van Tyne drifted further from McLaughlin, even opposing for a while the latter's speaking trip to England in early 1918. By the end of the war the philosophical rift between them had grown to such an extent that McLaughlin suggested they dissolve their partnership on the textbook, currently under revision. Their positions, he felt, were too divergent to compromise when writing about the war situation.[47] They somehow patched up their differences and Van Tyne allowed McLaughlin to write the bulk of the new material on the war. The revised text, particularly the section on the preparedness controversy of 1914-1917, displeased Van Tyne and in an angry outburst he complained, "I am utterly disgusted to have to stand for some of the things that are now in the text. I think it nothing less than shameful for one thing to rob Roosevelt of the credit for his splendid service in keeping awake the conscience of the nation when Wilson was giving it opiates."[48] In this case McLaughlin prevailed and Van

---

46 McLaughlin to Van Tyne, 8 March 1917, Box 1, Van Tyne Papers, Michigan Historical Collection, Rackham Building, University of Michigan.

47 McLaughlin to Van Tyne, 7 October 1918, in ibid.

48 Van Tyne to McLaughlin, 3 October 1919, Box 3, Folder 4, McLaughlin Papers, University of Chicago Library. Van Tyne was partly justified in his disgust. McLaughlin had portrayed the preparedness movement as menacing in its militarism. See A *History of the United States for Schools* (New York, 1919), p. 471.

Tyne was unable to extend his NSL loyalties into schoolbooks. While these ruptures over war issues did sully their personal relationship, their professional statuses rose to parallel heights for reasons independent of the war. Both Van Tyne and McLaughlin continued to head their respective history departments at Michigan and Chicago, and both became acknowledged authorities in their fields of Revolutionary and Constitutional history. Van Tyne's *The War of Independence: American Phase*, published in 1929, won a Pulitzer Prize and became for many years a standard reference. McLaughlin's *Constitutional History of the United States* (1935) also won a Pulitzer Prize and was acclaimed as a model of its kind. These disputes and accomplishments showed that personalities and reputations could react in an opposite manner to the war.

James T. Shotwell gave no indication of ever having become disenchanted with his wartime propaganda work, did not hesitate to add to his *Who's Who* credentials that he was the original NBHS chairman, and apparently felt no ill effects from the episode on his postwar career. When he recorded his memoirs in 1951 and later wrote his autobiography, he had come to the conclusion that the NBHS work was of minor influence. He originally regarded as important the pamphlets done in conjunction with the CPI, but upon reconsideration, changed his assessment to that of "lasting interest." In the same spirit he denigrated the importance of the NBHS historians in helping to mobilize public opinion: "I think the country swung in support of Wilson from the pressure of the event itself, rather [than] from the arguments of an academic, scholastic, and historical nature. . . . That may have affected the colleges and some of the intellectual reading public, but the mass of the people moved into the war from another motivation than that of our academic background of work."[49]   Shotwell's energies toward the end of the war had shifted from the NBHS to the work of the Inquiry, helping to prepare for the Versailles conference, and his later historical career displayed the same interest in diplomacy and peace movements. He was instrumental in discussions which

[49] J. T. Shotwell, "Reminiscences," Columbia Oral History Collection, Columbia University, p. 70.

led eventually to the Kellogg-Briand Pact of 1928, and during the Second World War worked in an advisory capacity with the Department of State concerning the United Nations. Even as an activist in public life he continued to function as a professional historian of wide renown, serving on the American Historical Association executive council and maintaining his reputation as a dynamic and popular Columbia professor until 1942. He edited more than 400 books, the most notable being the Carnegie Endowment's 150-volume *Economic and Social History of the War,* and wrote several works of lasting merit dealing with the Versailles conference and religious history.

Carl L. Becker was alone among the mobilized historians in disavowing his wartime propaganda work, yet it affected his career no more than it did the careers of those who defended their involvement. The quality of Becker's work was Wilsonian in its idealistic championship of the moral crusade against autocracy, and the president had commented favorably on one of his CPI pamphlets. The postwar peace conferences and the mutilated Fourteen Points destroyed much of Becker's faith in rational behavior and he regretted having been swept up in the war activity as one of Wilson's disciples. He lamented to a friend in 1920 that "What really irritates me, I will confess to you, is that I could have been naive enough to suppose, during the war, that Wilson could ever accomplish those ideal objects. . . . A man of any intelligence . . . should have known that in this war, as in all wars, men would profess to be fighting for justice and liberty, but in the end would demand spoils of victory."[50] As another decade passed, Becker's disillusion turned into cynicism, making him a passive ally of Barnes and the revisionists and showing just how far he had moved from his idealistic involvement in propaganda work. In a bitter essay, "Loving Peace and Waging War," he juxtaposed phrases that he had used as a pamphleteer with phrases which now struck him as closer representations of the truth: What had been a war for honor and defense of property rights now appeared as "millions of dollars in bad debts"; America's

---

[50] Becker to William E. Dodd, 17 June 1920, Box 15, Dodd Papers, Manuscript Division, Library of Congress.

much heralded attempt to make the world safe for democracy had, in Becker's new vision, "made the world safe for dictators."[51] If his public rejection of wartime propaganda work was an act of expiation, the profession required no penance and his career moved forward like a triumphal march. His reputation at Cornell as a skeptical intellect and an exacting prose stylist grew to legendary proportions, and his books, such as *The Declaration of Independence* in 1922 and *The Heavenly City of the Eighteenth Century Philosophers* in 1932, soon became classics. As president of the American Historical Association in 1931 he insured his place in the pantheon of American scholars with his famous address, "Everyman his own Historian," a provocative espousal of historical relativity.

Few historians of the war years were as public as Becker in revealing their disenchantment with war work or as adamant as Hart, Van Tyne, or Ford in defending it. Most kept silent or made their assessments so circumspect as to be uninformative. Historians can be loquacious when describing the motives and opinions of their biographical subjects and laconic when their own personal lives are concerned. Whether they regretted, defended, or merely forgot their propaganda work is a matter of conjecture. What is relatively certain, however, is that no matter what these silent ones felt about their work or what their critics said about it, their careers proceeded unaware. Evarts B. Greene and Dana C. Munro had both been chairman of the NBHS and pamphleteers for the CPI, and both accomplished their best scholarly work after the war. Greene went from Illinois to Columbia, where he displayed his versatility by continuing his work in American history and developing the Institute of Japanese Studies. He contributed one of the outstanding volumes to the History of American Life series, *Revolutionary Generation, 1763-1790*, and received from his colleagues in 1930 the presidency of the American Historical Association. Munro remained at Princeton and moved steadily upward in professional ranks, becoming American Historical Association president in 1925, managing

[51] Becker, *New Liberties for Old* (New Haven, 1941), p. 66.

editor of the *American Historical Review* in 1928-1929, and being recognized as the foremost American authority on the Crusades.

Wallace Notestein stated flatly a few months before his death in 1969 that his war work "had no effect whatever on my academic career," and the facts bore him out.[52] A lifelong Anglophile, he traveled, researched, and taught in Britain when he could take leave from his advancing appointments at Cornell and Yale universities. The publication of *The Winning of the Initiative by the House of Commons* in 1924 and *The English People on the Eve of Colonization* in 1954 serve as arbitrary parentheses for thirty years of valuable and respected writing following the war. Samuel B. Harding and Robert M. McElroy both fell into relative obscurity in the profession after the war, but this was a continuation of their prewar status and represented no radical change. Harding continued to do editorial work in children's literature and taught at the University of Minnesota until his untimely death in 1927. McElroy worked for Leonard Wood's presidential nomination in 1920 and published an authorized biography of Grover Cleveland in 1923. He spent the remainder of his active career through 1939 teaching in British universities and became somewhat peripheral to professional activities in America.

Even if propaganda work had managed to mar the reputations of some of the historians, it probably could not have touched that of J. Franklin Jameson. Like Hart, his influence in and on the historical craft was too prevading and illustrious to be shattered by a few months of patriotic enthusiasms, and he remained the "Ambassador of Scholars" until his death in 1937. He continued as managing editor of the *American Historical Review* until 1928 while helping to get under way publication of the monumental *Dictionary of American Biography*. When he assumed the directorship of the Library of Congress Manuscript Division in 1928 he used his many contacts to increase the government's archival holdings, not the least of which was the Henry Folger Shakespeare collection from his Amherst friend and classmate. The brass plaque within the National Archives today pays tribute to his role in

---

[52] Notestein to author, 27 August 1967.

making the Archives a reality and commemorates the long career which helped transform the study of history in America from the avocation of amateurs into the respected profession of scholars.

That their careers went largely untouched by their propaganda work does not diminish the fact that these historians undertook the work, that it stirred up ample criticism, and that it created personal and professional embarrassment. Much of the immediate criticism was more shrill and irresponsible than the propaganda being attacked, but one indiscretion does not cancel another. The body of their work stands as a reminder of one phase of America's war mobilization and is as deserving of evaluation as the Liberty Bond drives and the imprisonment of socialist agitators. The historians set precedents as scholars in service to an American war effort and hence had to set their own standards. If in their eagerness they believed that their efforts would help American democracy to triumph over the tangled problems of Europe and to create a better world for the future, they can be forgiven their happy illusions and dismissed as part of an idealistic age. If they consciously departed from their scholarly training and abused the canons of their craft in service to the state, then they must be held accountable for their breach of professional ethics.

Good intentions to the contrary, their propaganda work represented a severe break with scholarly historical standards. Accepting the fact that the degree of deviation varied among the CPI-NBHS-NSL historians, with the NSL generally being the least admirable, the work of all three groups departed from the canons of thorough research, objectivity, and dispassionate presentation. The worst of the CPI and NSL pamphlets contained classic examples of selective research, distorted meanings, misquotations, national prejudices, ethnic stereotypes, and impassioned writing. Much of the propaganda attempted to emulate scholarly work and made its charade even more glaring; the professional earmarks of footnotes and bibliographies were frequently as misleading as the texts they supplemented. The educational suggestions to schools and teachers represented dangerous experiments on impressionable minds. The NBHS construction of historical analogies often produced a perversion of both historical facts and current events, and the NSL's desire to rewrite Anglo-American history as an unbroken record of friendship represented an approach that could have turned history into a pliable tool to be manipulated according to present needs.

While some of the historians, such as Notestein, Greene, and Munro, agonized as scholarship turned into polemics, they soon acclimated themselves to the wartime transformation. The pamphlet files of the CPI are filled with rejected manuscripts, some of which were atrocious degradations of scholarship. The fact that Ford suppressed these items spoke well of his selectivity and indicated that the propaganda work could have been much less respectable than it was. This does not diminish the fact that many of the published items contained material that would not have slipped by a conscientious historian under normal conditions. Abnormal conditions were obviously present when Jameson and Harper gave their "sanction" to the Sisson Documents. Under the pressure of national policy these two men undertook a controversial project with inadequate time, language skill, and technical knowledge, and the results proved both unscholarly and embarrassing. Much of the propaganda work was creative, blissfully idealistic, and successful as a molder of facts to support a war, but it was poor history and should never have been paraded in that guise.

The unscholarly characteristics of much of the propaganda became even more obvious in light of occasional temperamental excesses on the part of the historians. Lapses in good judgment were almost inevitable since fear, intolerance, and inflated patriotism became by-products of the war, and government and extremist groups ferreted out disloyalty and prosecuted security risks with little restraint. But for historians to display the same lack of discipline as did those not tempered by the rigors of academic training and professional responsibilities made their actions even more indefensible. The internecine quibbling between the CPI and NSL historians brought honor to neither and drew to public attention indiscretions that might otherwise have gone unnoticed. When they accused each other's work of incompetence and dishonesty, they flaunted sophistic standards, for their own work would have failed the tests being imposed upon the competition. There is no adequate explanation for McElroy's angry outbursts and name-calling at the University of Wisconsin except that he temporarily gave way to irrationality when a situation went out of his control. This one excess—no matter how temporary—affected his subsequent speaking engagements and cast doubts on his emotional balance. Van Tyne fell into a similar breach of taste with his intemperate conduct during the *Two Thousand Questions and Answers* episode, thus raising questions about his editorial ethics, a problem that did not affect him before or after the war. By indulging in the excesses of the war years some of these historians were guilty of perpetuating the very myths, rumors, and shibboleths, such as hunnish stereotypes and simplistic casual factors, that years of scholarship had tried to erase. Atypical but damaging episodes such as these made many historians appear neither better informed nor less prejudiced than the untutored public whose opinions they were supposed to be guiding.

The war work was an aberrant chapter in their lives and was not repeated by them or another generation of historians in the Second World War. The *Mississippi Valley Historical Review* published an article soon after American entry which indirectly sounded a warning against a recurrence of the activity.[53] It reviewed some of the mistakes made by the CPI-NBHS historians of the previous war and commented that a historian cannot be expected to deny his citizenship or services in time of national crisis. This divided state of mind fell between the two stools of objective scholarship and patriotic service, thus typifying the dilemma and doing nothing to resolve it. World War II saw American historians working in many capacities for their government, yet did not see them mobilized into cadres of propagandists acting as "court historians." Elmer Davis's Office of War Information was not a repetition of George Creel's CPI and contained no subcommittee of historian pamphleteers and orators. Neither was there a semiofficial NBHS to serve as a clearinghouse for historians

[53] William T. Hutchinson, "The American Historian in Wartime," *MVHR* 29 (September 1942): 163-86.

wishing to participate in the war effort. When self-righteous demands appeared, approximating the NSL crusades, they came from organizations headed by figures other than historians. Both the major historical journals abstained from pushing any systematic historical participation in war work; they merely chronicled the activities of members who served in individual tasks. This paucity of organized historical activity reflected several factors: the manner of American involvement in the war did not necessitate scholarly justification and manipulation of public opinion; the greater sophistication of the communications media and citizenry and the comparative lack of chauvinism and hysteria precluded a revival of the simplistic propaganda of World War I; and the profession was more acutely aware of the dilemma facing it.

The dilemma prevails. Historians do not become "moral eunuchs" during a national crisis any more than do linguists, physicians, or engineers. Still, their efforts to aid their country with their particular expertise set them up for accusations of having sold their professional ethics and succumbed to an official doctrine. Whether their work of civic education is scrupulous or twisted, if it is done and disseminated for the government it is propaganda and the scholar's reputation is permanently suspect. Since World War I, historians have found it difficult to cross the barrier which separates professional scholarship from patriotic service without the fear of contaminated credentials. The craft of history since 1918 has become a very delicate art, producing a durable commodity only when cultivated in a political vacuum. The writing of history is laudable when the pursuit and presentation of past truths are for academic enlightenment; when used for pragmatic purposes, such as buttressing or publicizing a government policy, the commodity sours and the practitioner becomes a purveyor of his craft. Even if during times of peace the historian may flavor his writing with the current "climate of opinion," that same practice done for the state during a national crisis becomes a defensive manipulation of the truth and the guilty historian is not to be taken seriously.

This seems to be the unwitting legacy of the historians of World War I. They offered their services to President Wilson's noble crusade in an idealistic gesture of patriotic service. Just as postwar disenchantment turned idealism into a naive anachronism, so did scholarly reappraisals transform well-meant propaganda work into a historical transgression. A half-century has not lowered the barriers and perhaps this is for the best. History is easily distorted by passion and crisis and amateurs will ever be ready to make distortions for transient reasons. Professional historians would be well advised to protect history from the amateur rather than to join in the temporary violation of it. A nation can be better and less dangerously served than by having the guardians of its past lead the retreat from scholarly standards. Despite recent appeals from young historians to be allowed to wear two hats—scholarship and political activism—the unofficial taboo remains. History, since the CPI-NBHS-NSL mobilized it for war service, has been battle-shy, a fragile thing which does not eagerly serve national crises. Historians today have the choice of wearing the historian's hat to court respectability or the propagandist's hat to test the legacy of the Great War.

Bibliographical Essay

Propaganda activity by American historians during World War I has received only cursory scholarly treatment, most of which falls into either descriptive cataloging of wartime participation or "revisionist" attacks on Wilsonian advocates. The first comprehensive review appeared shortly after the war in the 1919 *Annual Report* of the American Historical Association, edited by Newton D. Mereness. Entitled *American Historical Activities during the World War* (Washington, 1923), it compiled articles concerning military, educational, and archival pursuits of historians, and provided rosters of local, state, national, and private agencies in which they worked. A recent analytical survey is the doctoral dissertation of Carol S. Gruber, "Mars and Minerva: World War One and the American Academic Man" (Columbia University, 1968), which covers the same ground with more depth but devotes attention to nonhistorians as well. Perhaps the most famous brief account of the subject is an article by C. Hartley Grattan, "The Historians Cut Loose," *American Mercury* 11 (August 1927): 414-30; here the author derides with considerable sarcasm the historians who "debauched Clio" with their propaganda work.

Most of the propaganda undertaken by historians was sponsored by three committees which are the primary concern of this book. The official records and publications of these committees offer the main sources of material. The records of the Committee on Public Information (CPI) occupy several hundred feet of space in the National Archives, Record Group 63, and provide invaluable insight into the mechanics of the official government propaganda organ. The files are arranged roughly by subcommittees and that of the Division of Civic and Educational Cooperation contains the records of Guy Stanton Ford's historians. Manuscripts, proofsheets, syllabi for lectures and slide-shows, and voluminous correspondence with many historians reveal the private actions of this well-publicized group. A congressional hearing in

June 1918 also reveals much information about the inner workings of the Ford group. Debating whether to continue financing the CPI, the House Committee on Appropriations summoned Ford and others to discuss their goals and techniques and the testimony (U. S., Congress, House, *Sundry Civil Bill, 1919: Hearings before Subcommittee of House Committee on Appropriations*, part 3, *Committee on Public Information*, 65 Cong., 2 sess. [Washington, D. C., 1918]) offers information not available in other published sources.

Publications of the CPI were in large part the product of Ford's historians and represent a significant portion of their work. The dozens of pamphlets (analyzed in chapter 3 above) demonstrate the level of scholarship used, the numbers of historians participating, and the general attitude of these men toward war issues. Attempts to influence public school curricula appear in issues of the *National School Service,* a twice-monthly newspaper supervised by Ford and Samuel B. Harding and distributed to teachers in autumn 1918. The official overview of CPI work is George Creel's *Complete Report of the Chairman of the Committee on Public Information, 1917-1918-1919* (Washington, D. C., 1920), which Creel soon expanded, exaggerated, and retitled *How We Advertised America: The First Telling of the Amazing Story of the Committee on Public Information That Carried the Gospel of Americanism to Every Corner of the Globe* (New York, 1920). In both of these accounts Ford either supplied the information or wrote the chapters dealing with the historians' work. The most exhaustive assessment of the CPI done by nonparticipants is *Words That Won the War: The Story of the Committee on Public Information, 1917-1919* (Princeton, 1939) by James R. Mock and Cedrick Larson. Although the authors attempt little more than catalog description, they generally sympathize with the CPI.

The National Board for Historical Service (NBHS) left a wealth of committee records befitting an organization of historians. Occupying thirty-five boxes in the Library of Congress Manuscript Division, the collection reflects the personalities of J. Franklin Jameson, who hosted the NBHS in his Carnegie Institution office, and Waldo G. Leland, the group's secretary-treasurer for its duration. The records are arranged according to the projects undertaken and intimate the historians' desire for consensus before taking public action. In addition to Jameson and Leland, James T. Shotwell, Evarts B. Greene, Dana C. Munro, and Joseph Schaefer are heavily represented in the correspondence files. The most systematic publishing venture of this group was a series of articles in the *History Teacher's Magazine,* representing the work of more historians than any other single project during the war. Beginning in September 1917, the series continued for nine months and allowed more than a score of historians to show how the war should be handled in the classroom. Leland summed up NBHS activity in the American Historical Association's *Annual Report* of 1919, already mentioned.

Activities of the National Security League (NSL) and its subcommittee of historians must be pieced together because the League left no single collection of records. The largest group of papers having direct relevance to the NSL is the Robert M. McElroy collection in the Library of Congress Manuscript Division. This collection is open for research, but unfortunately not for publication. His papers enhance but do not alter the information available in other sources. Another invaluable source is the congressional investigation of the League's financial and political affairs (U. S., Congress, House, *National Security League: Hearings before a Special Committee of the House of Representatives,* 65 Cong., 3 sess. [Washington, D. C., 1918-1919]). Lasting from December 1918 to February 1919, these hearings fill more than 2,000 pages with testimony from NSL officers and opponents and divulge information not available elsewhere. Of particular note is McElroy's hostility toward the congressmen and the investigation. Further official material from the NSL appears in its pamphlets, a series of articles by its historians entitled "The Battle Cry of Freedom" beginning in the February 23, 1918, issue of *The Independent,* and in the *NSL Bulletin,* a periodic newsletter written largely by or about McElroy. A three-part series by Arthur J. Nelson in the *Progressive Magazine* (June-August 1928) chronicles the basic history of the NSL and remains the most lengthy in print. Nelson's excessive criticism is somewhat offset in the more recent, brief, and objective account by Robert D. Ward, "The Origin and Activities of the National Security League, 1914-1919," *Mississippi Valley Historical Review* 47 (June 1960): 51-65.

Personal papers of a few historians proved indispensable. The J. Franklin Jameson Collection (Library of Congress Manuscript Division) is large and arranged alphabetically by topic and person, thus expediting research for correspondence between the many historians with whom Jameson kept in close contact. Several folders of Waldo Leland's letters are included in this collection, enhancing the material available for the NBHS. Guy Stanton Ford's papers (University of Minnesota Library) offer a personal supplement to CPI Records and include a copy of the five-volume oral reminiscences done for Columbia University in 1954-1955. The latter item is of particular value for comparing his recent assessment of the propaganda work with his earlier statements. The Robert McElroy Papers have already been discussed in relation to the NSL. Andrew C. McLaughlin's papers (University of Chicago Library) are of great help concerning the NBHS English mission of 1918. Included are the original drafts of McLaughlin's speeches, material ancillary to his CPI pamphlet, and other biographical items. Offering additional resources on the English mission are the Charles Moore Papers (Library of Congress Manuscript Division). The scrapbook clippings and the daily journal which Moore kept while he accompanied McLaughlin offer a rich commentary. The Samuel N. Harper Papers (University of Chicago Library) have relevance only to the controversial Sisson Documents, but in that respect are unmatchable. The drafts for Harper's memoirs contain several unpublished portions which reveal unusually personal testimony. Helping to fill out the slim resources on the NSL are the Claude H. Van Tyne Papers (Michigan Historical Collection, Rackham Building, University of Michigan). His wartime correspondence with McLaughlin, McElroy, and other historians, and the material involving NSL programs are pertinent.

Of lesser value, the following collections of personal papers helped supply tangential information and fugitive correspondence from other historian-propagandists: Carl L. Becker (Collection of Regional History, John M. Olin Research Library, Cornell University), Albert Shaw (New York Public Library), August C. Krey (University of Minnesota Library), Lawrence M. Larson (University of Illinois Library), William E. Dodd (Library of Congress), William Stearns Davis (University of Minnesota Library), George Creel (Library of Congress), George Burton Adams (Yale University Library), and Woodrow Wilson (Library of Congress). Especially disappointing were the unpublished oral reminiscences of Waldo G. Leland (Columbia University) and the James T. Shotwell Papers (Columbia University), neither of which contains much on this subject. Shotwell's oral reminiscences, taped during 1951-1952 at Columbia, provide more than his papers but are still thin on his propaganda work. Also disappointing are the A. B. Hart Papers (New York Public Library), which contain little of relevance to the war except a short typed reminiscence. Of the few principals still alive fifty years after the war, four offered their reflections on the historical propaganda in correspondence with the author; they were Wallace Notestein, Harry Elmer Barnes, Richard A. Newhall, and C. Hartley Grattan.

Published memoirs and autobiographies are rare and of limited use, proving that historians are largely an anonymous group. A few personal accounts did offer material collaborative to facts already known. The *Autobiography of James T. Shotwell* (Indianapolis, 1961), provided the same material (often verbatim) as his oral reminiscences and tended to denigrate the influence of historians during the war. Two articles by Carl Becker, "A Chronicle of Facts," *New Republic* 25 (23 February 1921): 382-83, and "Loving Peace and Waging War," reprinted in his *New Liberties for Old* (New Haven, 1941), pp. 44-75, show Becker's disillusion with wartime idealism. *On and Off the Campus* (Minneapolis, 1938) is a collection of Guy Stanton Ford's writings, one of which is an essay on his CPI work offering a brief supplement to his other statements. *The Russia I Believe In: The Memoirs of Samuel N. Harper, 1902-1941* (Chicago, 1945) covers Harper's participation in the Sisson Documents episode but must be read in conjunction with his unpublished memoirs. George Sellery's *Some Ferments at Wisconsin, 1901-1947* (Madison, 1960) sheds some light on the McElroy affair in Madison.

Debates in the *Congressional Record* illuminated several issues concerning the NSL and CPI, and the comparative documents printed there, especially those involving Van Tyne, greatly simplified research. Congressional hearings also revealed many details about historians that might otherwise have gone undetected. Already mentioned are the hearings on CPI appropriations and NSL finances. Another hearing drew testimony from A. B. Hart regarding pro-German organizations and propaganda activity. Hart's statements, although brief, were direct and revealing. See: U. S., Congress, Senate, *Brewing and Liquor Interests and German Propaganda: Hearings before a Subcommittee on the Judiciary*, 65 Cong., 2 and 3 sess. (Washington, D. C., 1919). Samuel Harding and Earl E. Sperry supplied additional information on historians and censorship in U. S., Congress, Senate, *National German-American Alliance: Hearings before the Subcommittee of the Committee on the Judiciary*, 65 Cong., 2 sess. (Washington, D. C., 1918).

Additional biographical material on the principal historians came from a variety of sources. Autobiographical studies and oral reminiscences are available for a few such as Shotwell, Ford, and Leland, and biographical tributes exist for Jameson, Ford, Van Tyne, and Becker. Details pertaining to private lives and academic careers also emerged from the *Dictionary of American Biography, National Cyclopedia of American Biography, Who's Who in America, Current Biography, Directory of American Scholars*, personal items in the *American Historical Review* and other journals, and obituaries in the *New York Times.*

Newspapers were of special value to this study, establishing chronologies, describing events, taking editorial positions, reprinting documents and pamphlets, offering forums for letters of which historians often availed themselves, allowing many historians to appear as guest columnists, and as a guide for congressional debate and hearings. The *New York Times* and its *Index* were basic and indispensable. Other papers of value in particular instances were the *New York Evening Post, New York Tribune, Christian Science Monitor, Wisconsin State Journal, Times* (London), and *Chicago Tribune.*

Periodicals and scholarly journals also offered considerable assistance both for contemporary source material and editorial counterpoint. The *American Historical Review* and *Mississippi Valley Historical Review* carried frequent news items, comments, and advertisements for historical propaganda, and several of the participants—especially Jameson—sat on the editorial boards. *The Independent and the History Teacher's Magazine* were channels for NSL and NBHS educational series, and the *Literary Digest* gave convenient assessments of popular opinion, so important to a study of propaganda. The *Minnesota History Bulletin, Journal of Modern History,* and *Wisconsin Alumni Magazine* offered help on specific topics. The *Atlantic Monthly* and *Dial* contained frequent articles and letters from historians, and the *Outlook, American Mercury,* and *New Republic* were articulate, if not always reliable sources of opinion. *The Nation* stands out for its quick definition of issues and its willingness to incite and reflect controversy.

Index

Adams, Charles Kendall, 5
Adams, Ephraim D.: and NBHS, 20; and NSL, 63
Adams, George B.: and intervention, 10; advice to Notestein, 45
Adams, Henry: as historian, 5-6; as prophet of change, 6, 9
Adams, Herbert Baxter: founding of AHA, 5; founder of historical seminar, 7-8
Addams, Jane, 9
Adrian, Mich., 48
AHA. See American Historical Association
Akron, Ohio, 64
Alabama, 120
"Alabama" claims, 41
Alaska, 41
Allen, William H., 92
Allied Maritime Transport Council, 72
Allies: threat to, 27; ideals of, 37, 42, 61, 69, 110, 117; and America, 38, 40, 42; and Russia, 98; mentioned, 67, 77, 114, 118
Alsace-Lorraine, 118
Altschul, Charles, 88
America at War, 50, 138
America Goes to War, 137
American Historical Association (AHA): leadership of, 2, 5, 24, 28, 71, 72, 141, 145-46; founding of, 4-5; meetings of, 8, 55; and *History Teacher's Magazine*, 110
American Historical Review: editors of, 3, 19, 71, 141, 147; founding of, 8, 28; and NBHS, 19-20; and *The War Message*, 54; and revisionism, 132-33
American Mercury, 137-38
American Nation series, 9, 28
American Political Science Association, 28
American Revolution: E. B. Greene on, 18; and Thomas Paine, 36; C. H. Van Tyne on, 41, 131, 144; and England, 70, 75; in textbooks, 88
American Revolution in our School Textbooks, The, 88

America's War Aims and Peace Programs, 41
Anderson, Frank M., 135
Ann Arbor, Mich., 8
Armistice: and NSL, 28, 97; and demobilization, 26, 126, 140; effect on education, 107, 119; mentioned, 101, 131
Atlantic Monthly, 82
atrocities: reported in *German War Code*, 46; demand for, 48; and *German War Practices*, 49; NBHS on, 67, 74; in *Two Thousand Questions and Answers*, 92; in *The Study of the Great War*, 117; in *Questions on the Issues of the War*, 119; mentioned, 134, 141. *See also* Bryce Report
Attila the Hun, 46
Australia, 89
Austria, 133
autocracy: versus democracy, 38, 64, 114, 121; attacks on, 67, 88, 145
Aydelotte, Frank, 118-19

Bagley, William C., 123
Baker, Newton D., 21
Balfour, Arthur: quoted, 74
Balkans, 112
Baltimore, Md., 58
Bancroft, George, 6
Barnes, Harry Elmer: on Shotwell, 17; on censorship, 88; and revisionism, 132-39
Battle Line of Democracy, The, 108-9
Beard, Charles A.: on war hysteria, 12-13; on intervention, 12, 16; *War Cyclopedia*, 52; mentioned, 31, 82
Becker, Carl L.: on idealism, 13; as pamphleteer, 41-42; *The United States: An Experiment in Democracy*, 88-89; and *History Teacher's Magazine*, 113-14; and revisionism, 135; later career, 145-46; mentioned, 14, 51
Belgium, 32, 48, 49, 91, 117
Berlin, University of, 18
Bernhardi, Friedrich von, 45, 51, 117